OTHER GREAT PRODUCTS FROM JAMES D KOFFORD

Visit aviationlogbooks.com to purchase the most comprehensive physical pilot logbooks available.

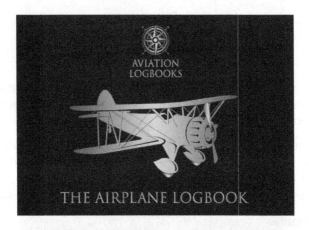

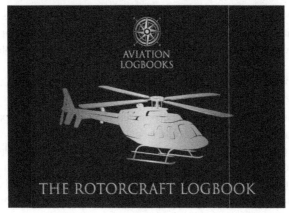

BECOMING A PILOT

What Every New Pilot Needs To Know To Save Time And Money In Flight School

JAMES D KOFFORD

CONTENTS

INTRODUCTION

"Once you have tasted flight you will forever walk the earth with your eyes turned skyward. For there you have been, and there you will always long to return."

— LEONARDO DA VINCI

Congratulations on choosing to become a pilot! You are about to start an incredible journey that will change your life for the better and will literally provide new perspectives on the way you view the world! Flight school will be a challenging process that will push you to become more than you are now as you develop knowledge and skills you will be proud of for the rest of your life.

A little bit about me. I have had a fun and challenging career as a professional dual-rated pilot including flight instruction, cargo, airlines, contract flying, and corporate aviation.

I have an undying passion for aviation and find happiness

in helping anyone and everyone who expresses an interest in becoming a pilot. I genuinely enjoy talking to those who are in your shoes now and watching them grow and learn about aviation.

I decided to write this book because I consistently spend hours giving people the advice you are about to read. It is my way of giving back to the aviation community by helping more future pilots than I could one-on-one.

This book is intended for those interested in the process of becoming a pilot, who are about to start flight training, and those already licensed but striving for additional licenses and are looking to streamline the training process. This includes both airplane and rotorcraft pilots.

My goal is to teach you how to independently take charge of your flight training while being as efficient as possible and provide you with the right mindset and motivation that will set you up for success. I will establish the guidelines and thought processes you will need to follow, cover the primary resources and references you will be using regularly, and explain how to use those resources and references to know precisely what to do and where to find everything you need.

If used properly, these practices will save you an incredible amount of time and can easily save you thousands of dollars over the course of your training. How much you save will be dependent on you and how diligently you follow my instructions.

Thank you for allowing me this opportunity to help you help yourself. I look forward to your success!

OVERVIEW, TERMS, AND DISCLAIMER

This book will start by first building a foundational knowledge of flight training. I will explain the critical first step you need to take before starting flight school, ideas to think about when finding the right flight school for you, and concepts you need to be aware of to set yourself up for success mentally and behaviorally.

From there, I will transition into an overview of the flight training, each license, and what you need to accomplish to obtain them while being as efficient with time and money as possible. I will then cover additional topics that will help wrap up the process and provide a condensed summary at the end for you to refer to as a quick reference guide to keep you on the fastest and cheapest path to success.

Aviation has multiple words and terms that mean either the same thing or are closely related but still used interchangeably. The following is a list of those words and phrases I use throughout the book.

- When mentioning only the ACS, I am referencing both the ACS and the PTS unless otherwise specified.
- Ground instruction is often reduced to simply "ground."
- Instructor and flight instructor are used interchangeably.
- Knowledge tests and written tests are the same.
- Licenses, ratings, licenses and ratings, or certificates are all different ways to infer ultimately the same thing. For simplicity, I will only reference them as licenses.
- Practical test and check ride are two names used interchangeably. Practical test is the formal name for the test, whereas check ride is the more common, informal name.
- The Federal Aviation Regulations are commonly called regs, regulations, FARs, or sometimes the F-A-Rs.

The following are all the acronyms used in this book for easy reference.

ACS- Airman Certification Standards
AFM- Aircraft Flying Manual
AIM- Aeronautical Information Manual
AME- Aviation Medical Examiner
ATP- Airline Transport Pilot
CFI- Certified Flight Instructor
CFII- Certified Flight Instrument Instructor
CFR- Code of Federal Regulations
DPE- Designated Pilot Examiner
ECFR- Electronic Code of Federal Regulations

EP- Emergency Procedure
FAA- Federal Aviation Administration
FAR- Federal Aviation Regulation
FOI- Fundamentals of Instruction
IGI- Instrument Ground Instructor
MEI- Multi-Engine Instructor
MEL- Multi-Engine Land
MES- Multi-Engine Sea
NAS- National Airspace System
PIC- Pilot In Command
POH- Pilot Operating Handbook
PTS- Practical Test Standard
R-ATP- Restricted Airline Transport Pilot
SEL- Single-Engine Land
SES- Single-Engine Sea

DISCLAIMERS

Everything in this book is current as of writing this (Nov 2022). Regulations and policies change from time to time. So does the format for how information is presented and from which resource. Some details may become outdated over time but are negligible as what I teach herein will give you the tools and ability to find the most up-to-date information at any given time.

Because of this, you should focus on the principles being taught, not necessarily the specific numbers or variables in the examples I use. If you understand and apply the principles I teach you, you will have no issue navigating any updates or changes that differ from this book.

Becoming A Pilot targets those training under the FAA (Federal Aviation Administration). However, there is still plenty of information for those training under other aviation governing agencies that will be beneficial. Nevertheless, the specific details such as tests, testing procedures, references and resources, regulations, and additional similar information may differ from the other governing agencies. Therefore, individual due diligence covering specific differences is required.

❧ 2 ❧
PREFLIGHT TO FLIGHT
SCHOOL

Before flying any aircraft, a pilot must conduct a preflight of that aircraft. A preflight is an inspection of the aircraft to ensure it is safe to fly.

Just like the aircraft needs to be preflighted by an entity other than itself, so does the pilot. This preflight comes in the form of an aviation medical conducted by an AME (aviation medical examiner) and generally happens annually.

Think of the medical as a non-invasive physical or general checkup. The AME will evaluate your vitals, vision, hearing, etc. They will also discuss your medical history, any medications you are using, or any health conditions you have.

Some medications or health conditions may temporarily or permanently disqualify you from obtaining a medical. Other medications or health conditions may allow you to qualify for a medical but with limitations.

There are three types of aviation medicals. First-class, second-class, and third-class. The cost of each of these will vary by the class of medical you get and which AME you go to.

Before starting flight training, <u>you should obtain a first-</u>

class medical whether or not your flight school requires it. This is because almost all pilot jobs require a first-class medical.

Some jobs will pay you to fly with a lesser-class medical. They are just fewer and further between and often come with more restrictions. In other words, not all pilot jobs require a first-class medical. However, a first-class medical permits you to work *all* pilot jobs.

To summarize, schedule an appointment with an AME to see if you qualify for a first-class medical before paying for any flight training. Doing so will be the first step in deciding if becoming a pilot is the right path for you.

❧ 3 ❧

CHOOSING A FLIGHT SCHOOL

There are many factors you should consider when choosing a flight school. The process can be daunting and overwhelming, but at the end of the day, it is a personal choice of what works best for you.

Where you get your licenses does not matter one bit regarding what the licenses will legally allow you to do. One place over another will not give you additional privileges or limitations with your licenses.

Some schools may offer additional perks outside of what the licenses allow you to do that may help in general, such as networking, pathway programs to various jobs, and other benefits, but that's about it. There is absolutely no difference in privileges and limitations of licenses from flight school A, flight school B, or even going to a flight instructor who teaches out of their garage and uses your aircraft to instruct you.

While there are many factors to consider when choosing a flight school, here are a few big-ticket items to consider.

- What is the hourly rate for the aircraft, and does that include the fuel and the instructor rate?
- What is the instructor's hourly rate?
- How many aircraft, instructors, and students does the school have?
- What is the networking potential?
- How long does it take for the school to return an aircraft to service after it goes down for scheduled maintenance?
- Will you have to pay upfront or pay as you go?
- What is the weather like year-round at the school's location?
- What happens if you have problems with the school you choose?
- Do they offer both Part 61 and Part 141 courses?

HOURLY RATES

You will be charged an hourly rate for every hour you fly, as well as every hour of ground instruction you do with an instructor outside of flying. These two items will be where the bulk of your money goes and, as such, matters most regarding the total cost of flight training.

So, if saving money by spending the least amount possible is a priority for you, getting the cheapest rate and completing training in the least hours is how to do it. Understand that these rates fluctuate with gas prices and the overall economy.

Most schools do their best to stay competitive. As such, the hourly rates will be similar between schools. If you like one school over another, but the school you want is a little more expensive, do not let that sway you from the school. Paying an extra few thousand dollars to go to the school that feels right for you will not make that big of a difference in the long run. It might feel like it right now, but not in the grand scheme of things.

Know your limits and what you are comfortable with regarding price differences. Some will be comfortable spending more than others.

The most important part is getting your licenses done and doing it quickly. Depending on your situation, it may be worth paying more to get your licenses done quicker since the sooner you get them, the sooner you will start getting paid to fly instead of paying to fly.

Take your time as you do your research, but within reason. Avoid the infamous analysis paralysis. Do not delay starting your training for months on end because you are getting hung up on comparing small details. Do your due diligence, make a choice, and get started.

AIRCRAFT, INSTRUCTORS, AND STUDENTS

The number of aircraft, instructors, and students a school has will play a large part in how frequently you can fly and conduct ground instruction. Generally, the lower the student-to-instructor ratio and the more overall instructors, the better.

You should be able to work with your primary instructor or another instructor as frequently as you need. It is incredibly frustrating when you want to fly or do ground instruction, but there are no aircraft or instructors available due to maintenance issues or a lack of staffing.

The school should accommodate you flying three to five times a week. That will get you through flight school at a great pace. It does not necessarily mean you will be flying that frequently each week, but it is good to know you can if you would like to or if it is needed. If you are striving to finish all your licenses between six months and a year, you will need to fly roughly that much or more.

NETWORKING

While getting an idea of how many instructors and students there are, you should also consider how many people you will interact with for networking purposes. The more people you get to know in aviation, the better, and for most individuals, flight school will be your initial primary source of networking in the aviation world.

Many pilot positions are filled simply by word of mouth and not posted publicly. This happens plenty with corporate aviation. One pilot will quit, and the remaining pilot(s) first seek out the people they already know and have enjoyed working with in the past before offering the position to the public.

I have been offered and became aware of multiple job opportunities by friends I made in flight school from both my students and instructors, and I have passed along opportunities to others as well.

The significant part about networking is someone else's network may differ from yours, so if you reach out to someone for assistance, even if they cannot directly help you, they may know someone else who can and vice versa. There will be more on the principles of interacting with others coming up.

MAINTENANCE DOWNTIME

Discuss the maintenance timelines when interviewing flight schools. The overall goal is to determine if aircraft will be available when you want to fly.

Talk with the staff and students at the flight school about the maintenance staffing. A red flag would be if the school continuously has issues staffing maintenance personnel.

Ask how often and how long aircraft are typically down

for specific maintenance tasks such as 100-hour inspections and overhauls. Different maintenance tasks take longer than others.

As you begin to ask around, you will find general ideas of how long each should take. Ask the staff as well as the students about this. The more people you talk to about periodic maintenance inspections, the better.

Schools sometimes exaggerate or provide hopeful but incorrect information about their timelines, whether intentional or not. The students who are driven and working hardest to progress will usually have a keen idea of the accurate timelines for the frequency and how long aircraft are down for maintenance at their school.

The primary concern is, will the aircraft be available when you want to fly so that you can reach your goals?

PAYMENT FREQUENCY

Paying upfront versus paying as you go.

Nowadays, some schools will have you pay for the specific course you are working on upfront, complete it, then pay for the next course, and so on. Others will have you pay as you go hour per hour, and some will give you the option. Knowing the payment structure will help you determine which financing path is best for you.

In the past, there was at least one flight school that required students to pay for all their licenses upfront. The school went under, and the students lost all their money.

As you can imagine, that would be incredibly devastating. Because of this, I would be extremely wary if you come across a school that requires you to pay for all your licenses upfront in one lump sum.

Do your due diligence and make sure you are comfortable with whatever the process is that the school uses.

WEATHER

The year-round weather at your school's location will play a large factor in how quickly you can get through flight school. It will also determine the quality of training you will get regarding weather and how to deal with it.

Those who have not been exposed to adverse weather while flying will quickly learn that there are some weather phenomena you want to avoid flying in or around. This is especially true with flight training when you are in the learning phase and using aircraft not equipped to handle adverse weather conditions.

The phenomena you do not want to fly in or around include the obvious, such as tornados, hurricanes, hail, and limited visibility from smoke or volcanic ash. But there are lesser obvious weather phenomena that you should use caution when flying in or around.

These include thunderstorms, clouds at altitudes with freezing temperatures, higher-altitude airports, especially when they have higher temperatures, areas with frequent high-speed winds, or flying near mountains on days with high winds.

Each phenomenon will affect your ability to conduct flight training safely. Luckily for you, when choosing a flight school, you can figure out what the annual weather patterns are at the school's location to see how much these phenomena will affect your training throughout the year. Either do some online research yourself or give the school a call and ask how many average days a year they are able to fly.

The better the weather year-round, the more days per year you have available to fly. However, before you drop this book to go sign up for a flight school in Arizona, there is something else you need to consider.

While Arizona averages roughly 300 days of sunshine a

year, doing your flight training elsewhere that has rapid and continuously changing weather patterns, such as Alaska or Hawaii, or locations that have all four seasons plus mountains to add an extra spin on the weather, such as Utah, Idaho, Montana, and others can be highly beneficial as well.

In such locations, you will face more real-world opportunities where you need to look up and use various weather products to assist you in making the go/no-go decision for your flight. These real-world repetitions will build more familiarization and a deeper understanding of the weather products with less effort involved, making your check ride that much easier.

Furthermore, these skills will carry over into your aviation career when you do not always have an instructor or another pilot to help you make the go/no-go decision.

I am not saying you will not get this knowledge if you train in a location such as Arizona. However, having to learn these tasks out of necessity to train versus a need to pass a check ride is entirely different.

Doing your training somewhere like Arizona will require more simulated scenarios to learn how to use the various weather products and make the go/no-go decision. As you can imagine, the quality of training may differ.

You will find that making the go/no-go decision is one of the most important things you will learn in flight school, and it is often much more challenging than you may think. Sure, it's easy when it's sunny, 70º, and there is light wind. It is also easy when there is a hurricane coming through the area. It is the gray areas that become a struggle.

It is one thing to determine if you are legal to fly with current weather conditions. But what happens when you include the forecast conditions into the picture?

What if you are legal to fly right now, but in an hour, it is forecasted to not be legal? Can you still go fly for 30 minutes?

Is that enough time to get quality training in? Is that enough time to takeoff and fly to a different location with better weather? What if you get stuck at another location due to the weather? You can start to see all the contingencies that come along with making the go/no-go decision.

How much better do you think you will be at making these go/no-go decisions when you do this regularly and see the clouds and the weather developing right in front of you versus someone improvising the weather by saying, "Your weather for today is [enter the scenario here], are you going or not going?" I hope you can see and process the difference.

I am all about getting through flight training quickly and efficiently. But I am also a big proponent of not cutting yourself short. Doing your flight training in Arizona or another similar location is perfectly okay if that is where you want to do your training.

You will still learn about all the weather products and get tested on them, and you can still understand the weather products to the same level as those who train elsewhere. It will just take more effort to ensure you spend the appropriate amount of time reviewing the weather products and going through various "gray area" scenarios to develop good go/no-go decision-making skills.

In short, if speed is of the essence, places like Arizona, with more average sunny days a year, are better than other locations. If you want to get really good at making go/no-go decisions with actual weather in not-so-obvious scenarios, find somewhere with more weather phenomena throughout the year.

There are plenty of places that provide a good balance. Or, you may not have a choice in the matter and are limited to wherever you live. There is nothing wrong with this. Every location will come with its own set of pros and cons.

Just remember, even though many factors can slow you

down, YOU will be by far the most prominent factor in how quickly you progress through flight training.

WHAT IF PROBLEMS ARISE?

What happens if you choose the wrong school, the school you selected does not provide what you need, or you run into issues with the instructors or staff that cannot be resolved? Most times, when you encounter a problem with your flight instructor or others in life, no one else will be aware of the problem until you address it. If you are harboring anger and resentment towards your instructor or anyone else because of something they did or are doing, they are probably unaware of the problem.

To resolve an issue, you first need to address it with the individual(s) you are having the problem with. Do this respectfully and calmly. Provide an opportunity and ample time for them to resolve the issue.

They will often be oblivious to the problem, and as soon as you bring it up, they will apologize and correct whatever needs correcting. If they are unable or unwilling to resolve the issue, that is when you escalate it to the next higher level within the organization.

Depending on the situation, you can determine how well the issue will be resolved based on how the person reacts when you bring it up.

The worst-case scenario would be having a problem with your instructor or flight school. You address the issue with your instructor, and they do nothing about it. You then escalate the matter to the staff or management and provide them an opportunity to rectify the problem, but there is still no acceptable resolution. This is when you would consider changing to another school if the problem is something you could no longer work with.

In the event you change schools, avoid burning bridges if possible. The aviation community is extremely small, and if you unnecessarily burn a bridge, there is a chance that it will come back to bite you later.

That said, at the end of the day, you must do what is best for you, period. If that means changing flight schools, then do so and do it professionally. It is possible to change schools cordially and without burning bridges. Be polite throughout the process and leave on as good of terms as possible.

Remember, where you get your licenses from does not matter. If you go to the most prestigious aviation school in the world versus going to your friend who will teach you for free, it does not matter.

So, if you do end up changing schools, don't fret. Your licenses allow you to do the same things no matter where they come from.

PART 61 VS PART 141

These two parts fall under the Federal Aviation Regulations and dictate how you get your licenses.

Think of them as two different paths you can take for each license. You can do your first license under Part 61, the following license under Part 141, back and forth, or you can do them all under one or the other, depending on what your school offers.

Earlier, I stated *where* you get your licenses does not matter. But *how* you get your licenses can make a difference.

Part 61 is the less restrictive of the two. Think of Part 61 as a baseline syllabus of minimum flight and ground hour requirements the FAA came up with for each license. Part 141 has differing minimum flight and ground hour requirements and stipulates that each flight school must develop an FAA-approved syllabus for every Part 141 course they offer.

Because of this, Part 141 courses generally require more ground and flight hours to meet the minimum requirements than Part 61.

Remember, you are paying per hour for all the instruction you receive in and out of the aircraft. The more hours required, the more money you will spend. Nevertheless, do not ignore Part 141 just yet.

Part 141 schools are typically associated with an accredited college. As such, the perks can include more opportunities for scholarships and grants, college credit, and potentially a degree, all of which affect finances, whether short or long-term.

If you are not completing flight school concurrent with a college degree, or you are going to a flight school that only offers Part 141 courses, there is only one real benefit of doing any of your flight training under Part 141. However, I will press the pause button for a moment to first explain some basics to better understand this principle.

Throughout this next part, remember that the focus is not on fully understanding all the ins and outs of the ATP or R-ATP license I am about to explain. The goal is to learn only enough about the ATP/R-ATP to know why you would want to consider choosing Part 141 over Part 61.

One of the licenses you will acquire well after initial flight training is airline transport pilot (ATP). There is a restricted version (R-ATP) as well. They are both the same license with the same privileges, except the R-ATP has minor restrictions on what you can do with the license. Hence, the R for "restricted."

Because R-ATP and ATP are considered the same license, when I only reference ATP, it includes R-ATP.

Due to the high flight hour requirements and the time it takes to obtain those hours, you will only become eligible for the ATP well after you have completed flight school. Yet, to fly for the airlines or other similar higher-profile jobs, you will eventually need one or the other. Which part you train under (Part 61 or Part 141) will determine which you can become eligible for.

Now that you know you will eventually get an ATP, you need to understand why you want to strive for the R-ATP instead of the ATP. The simple answer is time.

The primary attraction to the R-ATP is that it requires substantially fewer flight hours than the unrestricted ATP. Fewer hours required means less time to become eligible for the license. This means you can potentially get hired by a company and begin seniority with them that much sooner.

As of writing this, ATP requires 1,500 flight hours. However, the R-ATP can require as little as 750 flight hours for current and former U.S. military pilots. Or, if you are not a current or former U.S. military pilot, you can still qualify for the R-ATP in as little as 1,000 or 1,250 flight hours, depending on other specific requirements you meet, primarily the amount of college education you have.

Therefore, you can obtain the R-ATP with 250, 500, or 750 fewer flight hours than if you were to go for the ATP. The true benefit here is the *time* you save by not having to fly those additional hours.

If you needed to fly an additional 750 flight hours as a flight instructor or at another lower entry-level pilot job, it could take you well over a year, depending on how frequently you fly and the duration of each flight. Even 250 hours will still take a significant amount of time to acquire.

If your goal is to work for a company that runs on seniority (most pilot jobs do), being eligible for the position potentially one year prior or even a few months earlier can create an incredible advantage in your career. The sooner you start that dream job, the sooner your seniority begins, and the better your quality of life will be throughout your duration with the company.

Now that I have covered those details, I will press the play button and put it all together. Remember, the whole purpose of this is to figure out why you would consider doing any of your training under Part 141 instead of Part 61. Here it is. There are multiple paths you can take to become eligible for the R-ATP. Each approach has its own set of requirements. However, all pathways to obtaining the R-ATP (except for military pilots) require you to complete instrument AND commercial under an *approved* <u>Part 141</u> course. That is why you should consider Part 141.

Finishing the thought from earlier, if you are not completing flight school concurrent with a college degree or going to a flight school that only offers Part 141 courses, there is only one real benefit of doing any of your flight training under Part 141. That benefit is checking off one of the requirements for R-ATP eligibility by completing instrument AND commercial under an *approved* Part 141 course.

If you were to do either instrument OR commercial under Part 61, you would automatically disqualify yourself from the R-ATP and need to build the full 1,500 flight hours regardless of whether you meet the other R-ATP requirements.

One more detail. The instrument and commercial courses must be "approved" Part 141 courses to count towards R-ATP. Having these courses approved for R-ATP is more than the mere standard Part 141 certification process for the school to teach Part 141. Due to this, if you are interested in R-ATP, talk to your school to verify that their instrument and commercial courses are approved for R-ATP eligibility.

To recap, Part 61 is usually cheaper and quicker as it has fewer flight and ground hour requirements. Aside from military pilots, doing instrument AND commercial under an *approved* Part 141 course checks off one of the multiple requirements to become eligible for the R-ATP that doing under Part 61 would automatically disqualify you from.

Qualifying for the R-ATP can help you get to your dream job much sooner by reducing the required flight time by an additional 250-750 flight hours.

Both Part 61 and Part 141 have their pros and their cons. It is up to you to do your research and choose what is best for your situation.

Here is some additional food for thought. If you have not yet obtained an ATP but meet the eligibility requirements, many companies will hire you and cover the cost to get the license. Use this to your advantage.

If your career progression is such that someone else will pay for you to get the ATP, let them pay for it. Money not spent is more money in your pocket.

If you are flying rotorcraft, the ATP is not as big of a priority as it is for airplane pilots.

The ATP will generally be an additional item on your resume that can help you stand out against other candidates for the same job. However, I still recommend getting the ATP and doing so as soon as you qualify for it.

The reasoning is you will either still be flight instructing when you become eligible to take the check ride or shortly out of instructing. Either way, you will be sharper on the schoolhouse knowledge required to pass the check ride as soon as you hit the minimums, whereas the longer you wait after you qualify, the more you will have to study and relearn.

Therefore, the sooner you get it, the easier it will be, and if there is ever a chance you need to have the ATP, you may as well get it and do so when it is easiest.

One last time, if your school offers both Part 61 and Part 141, figure out which one requires the least amount of flight and ground hours per course if you want to go the cheapest and fastest route to get paid to fly. If becoming eligible for an

R-ATP to progress your career quicker appeals to you, you must look into the FARs for all the eligibility requirements to decide if it is worth doing instrument and commercial under an approved Part 141 course.

SUMMARY

In a nutshell, you are the one paying for the education you are getting. Just like college, you have the choice of what school to go to. Do your research, analyze the pros and cons, avoid analysis paralysis, and make your choice.

Keep in mind that you need to do what is best for you. If the school you initially choose is not providing what you need or there are serious issues that arise, you can always cordially and professionally change to another school.

❧ 4 ❧
YOUR INTERVIEW ALREADY STARTED

The aviation community is incredibly small. As of writing this, less than 1% of the world's population are pilots. While the actual number of certified pilots may be in the millions, in the grand scheme of things, it is a small world. The chances of you crossing paths with a pilot you met once at a fuel stop in the middle of nowhere are surprisingly high.

What does this mean to you? It means every interaction you have is potentially a job interview you did not realize you were having.

The interactions you have with anyone in the aviation world, or anywhere for that matter, have the potential to be the start of a great friendship, the introduction you need to get the job of your dreams, the ability to get back on your feet after an accident, or an employee you want to hire after starting your own business.

This is especially true when you start at a flight school. As soon as you earn your licenses, you will typically be interviewing for a slot as a flight instructor with that same school.

Remember, just because you paid the flight school for

your training does not mean you are entitled to or guaranteed a position as a flight instructor with them. Most schools will make you interview for the job.

Believe it or not, your interview does not start when they close the door of the office to conduct the formal interview after you have become an instructor. Your interview started a long time ago when you first reached out to the flight school on the phone or in person and continued throughout your entire flight training.

Your appearance, behavior, and attitude towards learning and those around you are watched and noticed by the instructors, office workers, other students, and anyone else you encounter.

Here are some tips and principles to apply to flight school and life in general that will help you nail the interviews you did not know you were having.

Show up for each ground or flight lesson on time. On-time means 10-15 minutes before a ground lesson's start time and up to an hour before flight lessons. This way, you can preflight the aircraft, fuel it, and take care of any last-minute needs.

Show up to each lesson prepared. Read the material you will be going over beforehand and have as clear an understanding of it as possible. Have any questions from your personal study written down and ready to be answered.

Be mindful of your appearance, body language, and verbal language from the get-go. Do not wear clothes with obscene words or gestures or full of holes. Wear closed-toe shoes. Practice good hygiene habits. Shower regularly, use deodorant, brush your teeth, cut your nails, and do not overdo it with strong scents like cologne or perfume. Trim up your beard and cut your hair. Keep your hair tidy and kept. Don't look like you belong on the streets, and don't show up having come straight from the gym without showering.

Befriend everyone you meet. Learn from those that are willing to teach and help those you can. On the same token, be aware of the people you spend most of your time with.

Perception is reality, and you are guilty by association, for better or worse. You evolve into and match the behaviors of those you surround yourself with most. Find people with good habits, expect more from themselves, and have a drive to constantly improve and socialize with them.

Do your best to be polite, positive, engaging, and as genuine with people as you can. Try to nurture your connections. Do not do it with the expectation that you will get something from them later in life. Do it with the intent of having an additional friend, maintaining a great connection, and with the hope that you will be able to help them out someday.

If you approach all your interactions this way, you will be surprised at how much more you will gain from each relationship than if you were to interact with people solely for your advantage and a "what can I get out of it" mentality.

I say these things for your awareness, for you to be conscious of your appearance and behavior, and to be the person you would want your future employers, employees, and coworkers to see you be. The same goes for the people you spend your time with.

There is a time and a place for everything. Be aware of your surroundings, pay attention to the activities you are doing, recognize the company you are with and around, and be honest with yourself as to whether your behavior and actions are becoming of a professional pilot.

Remember, whether you know it or not, your interview has already started, you are guilty by association for better or for worse, perception is reality, and first impressions last the longest.

✣ 5 ✣

INSTRUCTORS AND YOU: THE
GOOD, THE BAD, AND THE
BETWEEN

T ruth bomb. Not all instructors are created equally, just like your teachers in school. This is just how it is.

Students become instructors who then teach other students. The quality of the instructor will largely depend on the quality of the student they were. Think about that and let it sink in. That should put you into the mindset to be the best possible student so that you, in turn, will be the best instructor you can be. The principles I am teaching will help you accomplish this.

You can always ask for a specific instructor but may not get them. Nevertheless, you will always be able to choose what you do about the instructor you do get.

To give you the best chance of having a great instructor, you should research the flight schools, colleges, private flight instructors, or wherever you are considering ahead of time. Get some face-to-face time for an idea of what kind of instructors the school offers and if you will get along with them. Have the mentality that you are interviewing them because that is precisely what you are doing. You are hiring them to teach you.

While you are interviewing them, remember that they are also interviewing you and your potential to become a future flight instructor. Their appearance, body language, attitude, and actions will always say infinitely more than anything that comes out of their mouth. Same with you.

There will be some instructors who will have put more effort into their flight training while they were students than others. It is usually apparent who they are.

It is possible to get an instructor who will be the most fantastic, knowledgeable, empathetic, patient person who can teach anyone anything, can vary their teaching tactics to match the student's learning style, and can click with anyone. Conversely, some instructors are lazy and selfish and will milk you for all you are worth wasting your time and money. And, of course, there are plenty of instructors between both extremes.

To give credit where it is due, most instructors are fantastic, but it only takes a few bad apples to ruin a bushel, and it only takes one bad apple to waste a lot of your time and money.

If you have issues with the instructor you received, apprise the instructor of the problem and allow them the opportunity to rectify it. Most problems arise due to a lack of communication, and chances are one of the parties is unaware that the problem even exists.

Respectfully bring it up and address the issue head-on. Give the instructor the time and opportunity to resolve the issue. If this doesn't work, take it to the next level and request a new instructor.

Know the difference between a strict instructor and a bad instructor. Tough instructors may not be fun, but they are great and will push you to be better and hold you to a higher standard. Bad instructors show up late, fail to teach you critical concepts and practices, convince you that you need to fly more than you do to help them build their flight time on your dime, etc.

Keep your eye out for the latter and firmly but respectfully speak up if you get stuck with one.

Remember, you may not get to choose your instructor, but you can choose what you do about the instructor you get, and if it comes down to it, you can always change flight schools if needed.

❦ 6 ❧

MORE THAN JUST FLYING

I f you believe that flight school will only teach you how to fly an aircraft, you are greatly mistaken. There is much, much more than controlling an aircraft through the air.

You will find that flight school is very study-intensive. Instructors like to explain that becoming a pilot is 85% knowledge and 15% flying the aircraft. While these percentages are not a science, they will be close to how you feel as you progress through your training.

There are copious amounts of information you will learn along the way. Sadly, there is no Matrix to plug into to download the knowledge directly into your memory bank. As such, approach flight school the same way you would eat an elephant. One bite at a time.

There is only one way for you to learn what you need to know, and that is by putting in the work to absorb and learn all the information. It must be in your head, and no one else can do this for you.

Not only do you need to know all the information, you need to know where to find it. The most time and cost-efficient way to do this is for you to read all the information directly from the source. This will ensure you get complete and correct information, you know exactly where to find it later, and you will only pay for ground instruction when you need it.

Whether you plan on becoming an instructor or not, approach your studying with the notion that as soon as you finish flight school, you will become one and teach others everything you are learning.

Put in the work now to help you help yourself and others later. Study now to become the instructor you hope to have while you are in training. Doing so will help you in the long run whether you become an instructor or not.

There will be plenty of studying and long, time-consuming work for you to do. The level of success, the rate you get through flight training, and the quality of your education all depend entirely on you, with very few exceptions.

You will get out of flight training what you put into it, and the more you put into it, the better off you will be in more ways than you imagine.

OVERVIEW OF LICENSES

The initial licenses that pilots will obtain are as follows.

1. Private
2. Instrument
3. Commercial
4. Certified Flight Instructor (CFI)
5. Certified Flight Instrument Instructor (CFII)
6. Airline Transport Pilot (ATP)

The licenses for airplane pilots will differ slightly from the list above. Unlike rotorcraft licenses, airplane licenses differentiate between land vs sea and single-engine vs multi-engine.

Therefore, instead of just obtaining private as rotorcraft pilots do, airplane pilots can potentially get single-engine land (SEL) private, single-engine sea (SES) private, multi-engine land (MEL) private, and multi-engine sea (MES) private.

The commercial licenses for airplanes follow the same

breakdown. SEL commercial, SES commercial, MEL commercial, MES commercial.

Airplanes also have an additional instructor license, multi-engine instructor (MEI). This license works for both land and sea.

Instrument only needs to be done once in a land or sea, single or multi-engine airplane, and will count for single and multi-engine as well as land and sea.

Airplane pilots only need both land and sea licenses if their specific job requires it. Generally speaking, most airplane pilots will only focus on their land licenses first, and then once they are into their career, they may opt into obtaining sea licenses or vice versa.

Despite the differences in possible licenses for airplane pilots, the same guidance and techniques I teach herein will apply to any additional licenses not included in the six listed above. By the end of this book, you will know how to find the necessary information for each additional license and be familiar with the required steps to take and pass each additional check ride.

Back to all pilots. The standard progression you will earn your licenses is the same as listed above, although instrument and commercial may occasionally swap.

For airplane pilots, you will typically go through the single-engine licenses through commercial first and then work on the multi-engine licenses. However, that is not always the case and definitely not the only way to do it. There will be more on that in a later chapter.

Each license allows you to operate aircraft with specific privileges and limitations.

To keep things simple, private will enable you to fly for fun with other people in mostly good weather, and with limited exceptions, you cannot get paid to fly. Instrument primarily allows you to fly with limited visibility, such as flying through clouds, and provides access into new airspace that private pilots cannot fly in. Commercial has the same privileges as private, but now you can get paid to fly. CFI allows you to teach private, commercial, and CFI. CFII will enable you to teach instrument and CFII.

This list is by no means inclusive of the privileges and limitations for each license, but it is a good layman's summary to get the ball rolling.

To get the licenses listed above, you will need to build up ground and flight knowledge. The ground knowledge will consist of topics such as aerodynamics, weather theory, aviation law, etc. The flight knowledge consists of learning how to fly the aircraft and handling it throughout various flight maneuvers.

GROUND KNOWLEDGE

Due to the similarities in categories and topics of information, the licenses listed above can be split into the following two groups.

GROUP 1	GROUP 2
Private	Instrument
Commercial	CFII
CFI	

Group 1. The topics you will need to learn for private are the same topics you will need to know for commercial. They are also the same topics you will need to know for CFI. With two exceptions, once you have learned everything you need to

know for private, you will not need to learn anything new for commercial or CFI. Your level of comprehension of the topics you learned in private will only need to become better with each progressing license.

The exceptions are you will learn one additional topic in commercial that you did not learn in private. You will also learn an additional topic in CFI that you did not learn in private or commercial.

Group 2. The same principle applies to instrument and CFII. Once you have learned all the topics for instrument, you will know all the topics for CFII and will only need to have a better comprehension of those same topics.

Therefore, you will primarily learn new information only during private and again during instrument. The other licenses will mainly be a review of the information you learned in private and instrument, which will help you better understand that information.

The airplane pilots will have a third group not included in the illustration above for the multi-engine licenses. However, despite having new information to learn with this group, most information from the previous licenses will carry over. As such, there is much less information to learn with this smaller third group than the first two groups.

The most significant difference between private and commercial compared to CFI, or instrument compared to CFII, is the expectation for you to teach the information. This emphasizes the importance of having a solid understanding of the information.

FLIGHT KNOWLEDGE

Flight knowledge is more clear-cut and divisive than ground knowledge, but it can still be broken up into the same two groups of licenses as before, as there are primarily two groups, or styles, of flight maneuvers you will need to learn.

GROUP 1	GROUP 2
Private	Instrument
Commercial	CFII
CFI	

Group 1. The flying in group 1 includes a variety of maneuvers that demonstrate proper control and handling of the aircraft in various scenarios and phases of flight.

While you will need to perform many of the same maneuvers for all three licenses in group 1, some maneuvers are only necessary for one or two of the licenses but not all three.

Sometimes, the maneuvers only need to be demonstrated to you instead of executing the maneuvers yourself.

Furthermore, the tolerances allowed for each maneuver may change based on the license you are working on. Generally, the higher the license, the more strict the tolerances become.

I will teach you how to determine which licenses require which maneuvers and what the tolerances are later.

Group 2. In group 2, the type of flying and the maneuvers you will perform in instrument will be the same for CFII.

Some maneuvers carry over from group 1. However, group 2 focuses more on flying the aircraft using your instruments within the flight deck instead of using outside references. This is because the emphasis in instrument and CFII is to fly approaches to landing with limited to no visibility as if you were flying through clouds.

The further you progress in your training, the more you will see this division in the grouping of the licenses.

Now that you have a better understanding of how the licenses are divided into two groups based on the required ground and flight knowledge, I will go over the tests you will be taking.

❧ 8 ❧

TESTING COMPONENTS OF A LICENSE

There are two required FAA tests you will need to take to obtain each license under Part 61 and Part 141. They are the knowledge test and the practical test. The practical test is more commonly known as a check ride.

Not all licenses require a knowledge test, but all will require a check ride.

Additionally, stage checks are required for Part 141 courses. Occasionally, Part 61 schools will require stage checks as well, but not often.

The knowledge test is a proctored, written, multiple-choice test you will take at a designated testing facility with an associated fee paid to the testing facility.

Most licenses only require one knowledge test, but CFI may need two, depending on a few variables. Similarly, a knowledge test may not always be required. These exceptions occur primarily within the instructor licenses.

The check ride is conducted by a designated pilot examiner (DPE) who is a representative of the FAA and has an associated fee that gets paid directly to the DPE. The check ride consists of an oral evaluation and a flight evaluation.

The oral evaluation consists of scenario-based questions incorporating the ground knowledge you learned throughout the license you are testing for. Your level of comprehension of the subjects tested will be commensurate with the license sought.

Think of the group 1 licenses. Both private and commercial cover the same material, but your comprehension of the material will be at different levels based on which license you are working on. If you are working on private, the DPE will hold you to private standards instead of commercial standards even though they both more or less test the same information.

The flight evaluation tests your ability to safely manipulate the aircraft through various maneuvers to a specified standard while maintaining situational awareness and accomplishing all required tasks. The standards to which you will need to perform the maneuvers are again commensurate with the license you are working on. The oral questioning can and usually does continue throughout the flight as well.

A stage check is a periodic, in-house mock check ride that tests your progression throughout each license. Aside from being required for Part 141, these stage checks are a way for the school and your instructor to ensure you are progressing appropriately, allow you to experience and help overcome the stress that often accompanies a check ride, and reduce the chance of failing the check ride.

The only prerequisite for the knowledge test is an endorsement from an authorized instructor verifying you are prepared to take the test. Once you have received the endorsement, you may take the knowledge test any time you want, but you must complete it before taking the check ride.

There are many prerequisites before taking the check ride,

including an endorsement. I will discuss the process of how to look those requirements up later.

Each flight school will set up the prerequisites for the stage checks. Refer to the school's course syllabus for details.

The knowledge test requires a specific score to pass. The check ride is pass or fail. You must pass the oral portion of the check ride to move onto the flight portion, and you must pass both the oral and the flight portion to pass the check ride. The stage checks are generally pass or fail as well. Again, the flight school will have specific details on those.

Suppose you fail the knowledge test or fail either the oral or the flight portion of the check ride. In that case, you must receive additional training on the areas you were deficient, obtain a new endorsement from an instructor, and then you may retake the knowledge test or check ride as needed. Many schools set up their stage checks the same way.

Stage checks are much less formal than a check ride. Nevertheless, take them just as seriously as you would a check ride.

You may retake knowledge tests, check rides, and stage checks as many times as it takes. However, the higher your test scores and the fewer failures you have, the better.

Think of these tests like your high school report card and you are trying to get into various colleges. The higher your GPA and the fewer failures you have, the better it looks.

Many companies ask about your knowledge test scores and any failures you have had, including stage checks. The fewer failures you have and the higher your test scores, the better you look on paper.

Set yourself up for success by putting in the necessary work to get the highest possible knowledge test scores and to pass each stage check and check ride on the first try.

❦ 9 ❦
PROGRESSING THROUGH TRAINING EFFICIENTLY
PART 1
FLYING

The most crucial task in flight training is to stay focused on your long-term goal of getting paid to be a pilot.

Flight training is the learning phase where you pay a large sum of money to learn how to fly. Assuming you do not want to spend more than necessary, you will want to get through the learning phase as quickly and efficiently as possible to reach the getting-paid-to-fly phase.

This process warrants completing all the required tasks in the least number of flight and ground hours possible. To do this, you need to be aware of the requirements for the licenses, find the path you want to take to complete those requirements, and come up with a list of all the tasks you want to accomplish during each flight before getting into the aircraft to maximize productivity.

From there, you must adhere to a high frequency of flying and studying to check off all the requirements and build proficiency in your maneuvers and ground knowledge. With that said, this will be a marathon and not a sprint. Find a sustainable pace and make it happen.

This chapter is split into two parts, as there are two halves to your training for each license. Each half is equally important, and both happen simultaneously. The first half comprises the flying requirements and proficiency with flight maneuvers. The second half is obtaining all the required ground knowledge and taking the applicable knowledge test.

I am going to discuss the following three topics within the realm of flying.

1. Eligibility vs proficiency
2. Accomplishing the requirements first
3. Looking ahead at the requirements for all of the licenses, not just the license you are working on now

ELIGIBILITY VS PROFICIENCY

Each license has a list of flight and ground requirements that must be met, including the knowledge test, to become eligible for each check ride. There will also be a list of flight maneuvers you must be proficient with and perform to a specified standard.

I will teach you how to find these requirements and standards in a later chapter.

For now, you need to be aware that just because you complete the requirements and are *eligible* to take a check ride does not mean you are *proficient* enough to pass the check ride.

Being eligible and being proficient are two different things. You need to meet the total time, check off all the flight and ground requirements, *and* you must be proficient in the maneuvers to take and pass each check ride.

Becoming eligible is simply a matter of meeting all prerequisites and checking off all the requirements. I will teach you how and where to look up the requirements for each license in another chapter, but I will teach you the order to accomplish the big-picture items a little later in this chapter.

Regarding proficiency with your flight maneuvers, it all comes down to you and how fast you pick up what will become the basics of flying. The faster you can learn the basics, the easier it will be for you to check off the requirements earlier on with each license.

Each license will introduce some new concepts you will need to build a base level of proficiency with to help you complete the requirements before focusing on proficiency only. This process should get quicker and easier with each additional license as your overall handling and understanding of the aircraft improves.

A key factor in building proficiency is frequency. Flying is like learning how to ride a bike in the sense that if you only practice for 30 seconds once a week, it will take you a lot longer and more total time practicing compared to spending hours a day every day.

Those who fly less frequently typically need more total flight hours to reach the same level of progression and proficiency as those who fly twice as often.

Flying is a perishable skill. Even more so when you are initially learning, as such, fly as frequently as you can while ensuring your ground knowledge progresses proportionately.

An incredible supplement to flying is taking advantage of chair flying. Chair flying is exactly as it sounds. You sit in a chair and pretend to fly as you go through various flight maneuvers and procedures. Doing so is a great way to practice anything you want to go over more.

Chair flying will help you build muscle memory with where your eyes need to focus, where and what your hands and feet will be doing, and help you to remember the order of events. As you do this, close your eyes and imagine where every switch, lever, and control is. Go through the motions in order as you work your way through each task and maneuver along with how the aircraft will respond. If you have a poster of the flight deck of your aircraft, hang that up somewhere in view as a visual reference to help out.

The goal is to imagine every step you are going to take in great detail, what the aircraft is going to do with each input you make, and what response you will see and feel.

For example, if you pull back on the yoke or the cyclic, how will the aircraft respond? What happens to the airspeed? What happens to the altitude? Where are you going to look to see those indications? What will you feel and see to verify the aircraft is doing what you want it to do?

Chair flying will help you get repetitions of anything you need additional practice on while not paying for the engine to run or for an instructor to sit beside you.

Compared to being in an aircraft where everything happens simultaneously, this allows you to slow everything down and take things one step at a time. The best part is you can do as many practice runs as you would like, and it doesn't cost you a cent!

You might be thinking this sounds stupid, and you are going to look like an idiot. Don't worry, you will. But don't let that dissuade you. Chair flying will save you a lot of money and make you a better pilot. And if it helps, every other pilot that cares about their training does the same thing.

Another helpful tip for increasing proficiency is attaching a camera inside the aircraft to record your flights. If you do this, ensure the camera's field of view can see both pilots, the instruments, and outside the aircraft. You can even connect audio to listen to the radio calls and review anything your instructor taught you during the flight.

You can pause, rewind, and review everything that happened as many times as you need to. In essence, you are getting multiple flights for the price of one. This process will help you learn from your mistakes, reinforce good habits, and help with your chair flying.

While this is a great tool to supplement your learning, be mindful that some schools will not allow cameras in their aircraft. There are many reasons for this.

One such reason is people tend to do things they otherwise would not, or should not, do as soon as a camera gets turned on. Another is it can be a massive distraction, which can quickly become life-threatening.

Here are my words of caution towards using cameras in the aircraft while going through flight training.

If you plan to use a camera, use it for the right reason. It is a training tool, that is it. Do not use the camera with the intent to gain popularity on social media while in training. Doing so is just asking for trouble.

The last thing you want to do is film yourself unintentionally doing something illegal, post it to social media, and then find out the hard way that what you did was illegal and have your licenses suspended or revoked. Or worse, you become so distracted by the camera for one reason or another that you crash the aircraft.

The last notable item to mention for proficiency is you need to be efficient with your flight time during each flight.

Think ahead and figure out precisely what you want to do and accomplish for each flight *before* getting in the aircraft. Come up with more tasks than you can do within the allotted flight time.

Ensure you brief your instructor on the plan *before* the flight so they can help facilitate it. Wasting time coming up with tasks to do while in the aircraft with the engine running costs you money. You pay for every minute the engine runs, so use every minute productively.

ACCOMPLISH THE REQUIREMENTS FIRST

As you proceed through your training for each license, accomplish the requirements first and then focus on increasing your proficiency with the maneuvers and anything else you want to work on second.

Ideally, you would do this in the same or fewer flight hours than the minimum total hours required for the license you are working on. Doing so will be the least expensive and most helpful when it comes time to schedule your check ride or reschedule it if necessary.

If the only remaining tasks you have before taking a check ride are obtaining the minimum required hours and/or working on proficiency, you will have the greatest control and flexibility over your remaining flights and flight schedule leading up to the check ride.

Setting yourself up this way gives you the choice to continue flying, which costs money but keeps your proficiency and confidence high. You can temporarily pause your flying and then do a refresher flight or more just before the check ride, which saves you some money. Or you can choose not to fly until the check ride to save the most money, but it would be the equivalent of icing the pitcher (or you, in this case).

The perk here is you have options and more control over what you can do. If that was not enough, there are fewer variables with proficiency flights than most requirement flights. Because of this, they are easier to accomplish and more likely to happen when you want them to, as there are fewer chances of a delay.

Conversely, if you still have requirements to meet as you approach your check ride, you lose some control and flexibility with how often or if you need to fly. The requirements must be met. Therefore, the required flight(s) must happen.

Requirement flights mean dealing with more variables outside of your control that are harder to mitigate than when working with a proficiency flight. This means potential delays for unknown durations.

The worst time to lose this control is within a week or two before a check ride, as your chances of rescheduling the check ride increase. Rescheduling can cost you more money and will likely increase stress.

Depending on the examiner's availability, weather, aircraft maintenance and availability, and other factors, you could push the check ride back a day or two if you are lucky, or it could be another three or more weeks if you are not.

A lengthy delay will buy you time to finish the requirements, but it also means you will likely pay more than you otherwise would, as you will most likely want one or more proficiency flights before the new check ride date.

The absolute last thing you want to have happen is start the check ride, pay the examiner fee, and then realize you have not met all the flight requirements. Although rare, it does occur.

In this instance, you would get a discontinuance, and the check ride stops wherever you were in the process. A discontinuance is neither a pass nor a fail. However, you would need to schedule another time to finish the check ride, which could be a day or two later or three or more weeks, just as before.

Whether you reschedule with the same examiner or a different DPE, you will get credit for the items you previously passed and pick up where you left off to continue the remainder of the check ride.

With a discontinuance, you will have 60 days to complete the requirements and finish the check ride. If you do not meet the timeline, you will start the check ride from the beginning, no matter who you do the check ride with or how far along you were before the discontinuance.

Depending on the situation and the examiner, you will most likely pay the examiner fee again, which you clearly want to avoid.

These scenarios are easily preventable if you ensure you finish the requirements first and then work on proficiency second.

With that said, while knocking out the requirements before working on proficiency is ideal in a perfect world, in reality, it is not always possible. There needs to be a baseline level of experience and knowledge that comes from proficiency flying to complete the requirements. Because of this, you will likely work on some proficiency items before you can check off the requirements.

You will find this to be the most true while working on private due to the number of new tasks you will learn simultaneously. Nevertheless, the process of completing requirements before proficiency should get easier with each progressing license.

You may be thinking that you won't be the person who leaves a requirement until the end. However, it unintentionally happens much easier than you would think due to the variables of flying. Pay attention as you progress, and if needed, slow down the proficiency flying to ensure you complete the requirements earlier on.

LOOKING AHEAD

Another primary factor in completing the requirements first and working on proficiency second is looking ahead at the requirements for *all* the licenses, not just the license you are working on now. More specifically, the minimum total required flight time for each license.

As you read through the regulations, you will find the following requirements. Private requires you to log 40 total hours of flight time as a pilot regardless of whether you are a helicopter pilot or an airplane pilot. Instrument does not have a specified number of total hours logged as a pilot. Commercial requires 150 hours of total flight time for helicopter pilots and 250 hours for airplane pilots. CFI and CFII do not have a minimum total time required as a pilot.

So what does this mean for you? It means you now know you have to pay for at least a minimum of 150 or 250 flight hours, respectively, to get through flight school. It also gives you a goal to shoot for, which I will discuss momentarily. Lastly, if you go over the 40 hours required for private or use more than the minimum necessary hours for instrument, it is not the end of the world since you will have to pay for those hours anyway to finish flight training. However, you should still strive to complete private and instrument in the minimum time possible if you are looking to save time and money. This is where that goal I mentioned comes into play.

The fewer flight hours it takes to complete private and instrument and to prepare for commercial, the more hours you will have that you already know you have to pay for to get ahead in the rest of your flight training. The further ahead you get in your training, the fewer hours you will need to pay for beyond the 150 or 250 flight hours required for commercial.

In other words, if you were completely prepared for the commercial check ride other than having the 150 or 250 total flight hours for eligibility, you could then pause your commercial license training and use the remaining hours to get ahead and prepare for as many additional licenses as possible.

If you learn quickly and are efficient with your flight time, you can complete almost all of your flight training within the 150 or 250 total flight hours. While this will not be a reality for everyone, this would maximize efficiency and should be the goal to strive for. The closer you get to this, the more money you will save.

No regulation states that you cannot work on other licenses while you build your total time for eligibility to take the commercial check ride. Nevertheless, completing requirements and practicing maneuvers for a license ahead of what you were initially working on is out of the norm. Because of this, some schools and instructors may not allow it. Nevertheless, it is entirely legal.

Keep in mind that it takes a solid understanding of the process and the ability to categorize and differentiate which tasks go with which license to keep everything straight in your head.

Because of this, it can be easy to get distracted with the process, lose sight of the first goal of preparing to take and pass the commercial check ride, and end up aimless, which would be a colossal waste of time. The checklists you will learn about in a later chapter will help reduce the chance of this happening.

This process also takes a willing instructor to help you work ahead. Again, this process may not be a reality for all.

That said, I will teach you the best way to go about this. Again, this process is all about how to use the flight time between instrument and obtaining the 150 or 250 total flight hours to become eligible for the commercial check ride.

The goal is to prepare for and study the necessary material, complete the flight requirements, and gain enough proficiency in the required flight maneuvers for as many of the remaining licenses as possible before taking the commercial check ride. This way, when you reach the 150 or 250 respective flight hours, you will be ready to take as many check rides as possible in the least amount of additional flight hours.

I will break this down for the helicopter pilots and then airplane pilots.

HELICOPTER PILOTS

The first step is to complete private and instrument. Then, prepare for the commercial check ride by studying the necessary material, meeting the flight requirements, and gaining proficiency in the required maneuvers. After becoming prepared to take the check ride minus the required 150 total hours, press pause on your progression with commercial to then turn your focus onto CFI to do the same tasks and then repeat for CFII.

Much of the preparation for CFI and CFII is ground knowledge. Thankfully, this does not eat into the 150 hours of flight time required for commercial, but it will still take a significant amount of time overall. Therefore, you may need more time to be completely ready for the CFI and CFII check rides while building the flight time to become eligible for the commercial check ride. That's okay.

The goal here is to knock out as many of the requirements and become prepared for as many check rides as possible so that you have less you need to do once you pass the commercial check ride. The less you need to do, the more money you will save.

The airborne requirements for CFI and CFII are the same maneuvers you did in private, instrument, and commercial. However, now you will fly them from the left seat instead of the right. Swapping seats throws you off more than you would imagine and takes time and practice to get used to.

Your instructor will also act as a new pilot who will intentionally perform maneuvers incorrectly that you need to identify, intervene, and correct. That may sound daunting, but it is actually a lot of fun!

Once you have prepared for the CFI and CFII check rides, or you are getting close to the 150 total flight hours required for commercial, stop working on CFI and CFII and focus solely on the commercial check ride. Use the remaining time to ensure you are comfortable and proficient with the maneuvers from the right seat again, and then take the check ride.

If you were completely prepared to do this, after you pass the commercial check ride, you could turn around and take the CFI check ride the same or the next day, followed by CFII.

If you need more flight time, or time in general, to prepare for CFI and CFII, no worries. Take the necessary time to prepare for those. However, if you are on top of everything and feeling ready for CFI and CFII, you may take those check rides back to back after the commercial check ride.

As you can see, if you maximize this process, the only flight hours you would pay for beyond the 150 required for commercial are any proficiency flights you still need or would like before taking the CFI and CFII check rides and the flight hours used in those check rides.

Again, not everyone will be able to do this. Nevertheless, if you can, this is the most efficient use of your flight time. If you take more than 150 total flight hours as a pilot to prepare for all your check rides, it does not mean you have failed. It only means you will pay for additional hours beyond the 150 required for commercial, which is fine and normal. However, the more prepared you are for the CFI and CFII check rides before reaching 150 hours, the fewer total hours you will need to become ready and the more money you will save.

If you decide to pursue this route, continue to study and review the commercial ground knowledge while working on CFI and CFII. Do not let that knowledge fade away as you progress beyond commercial while building up to 150 total hours.

Please remember that the priority goal is to ensure you are prepared for and ready to pass the commercial check ride BEFORE working on CFI and CFII.

There is no point in working on CFI and CFII if you are not already in a position to pass the commercial check ride.

Passing the commercial check ride is the first gate you must pass through.

Take it one license at a time if you need to, but if you understand what I am teaching you here and you are feeling good about it, have at it!

AIRPLANE PILOTS

Alright, airplane pilots, your turn. Your path will be similar to the helicopter pilots. However, you have more required total hours (250) before being eligible to take the commercial check ride, more licenses, and more options, which makes it more beneficial and also slightly more confusing.

I am going to use two scenarios to explain this.

The first scenario assumes you will reach the 250 total flight hours required for the eligibility to take the commercial check ride sometime before completing the flight requirements and gaining the necessary proficiency for all the remaining licenses. However, the catch here is you will not know ahead of time where you will be in that process when you get close to 250 total hours. Because of this, the order of licenses you will work on here will be more thought out and deliberate to simplify your studying and help put you into a position where you can get paid as a pilot sooner rather than later.

The second scenario is the route you would take if you knew ahead of time that you had enough flight hours to accomplish the requirements and gain proficiency for all the licenses before reaching 250 total hours. In this scenario, the order in which you progress through the licenses really does not matter. The only benefit of doing them in a specific order is to help keep the knowledge and tasks straight in your head.

Both scenarios assume you are starting with single-engine licenses first, as it is the most common progression for airplane pilots. If you begin training in a multi-engine airplane, swap out each single-engine reference with multi-engine, and the rest of the process remains the same. Land versus sea only matters if you are doing both simultaneously. If you are doing them simultaneously, I wish you the best of luck, as I will not be going down that rabbit hole here.

Side note. Pilots are only required to obtain one of the five possible private pilot licenses as they progress: SEL, SES, MEL, MES, or helicopter private. Because of this, you do not need to do private and commercial for single-engine and then private and commercial for multi-engine, or vice versa. Once you have a private pilot license, you can then go straight to any one of the commercial licenses, including helicopter commercial, if your heart desires.

For example, if you completed single-engine private, you can skip multi-engine private and go straight to multi-engine commercial. Or, if you started with multi-engine private, you can skip single-engine private and go straight to single-engine commercial. Additionally, if you have completed helicopter private, you can go straight to single or multi-engine commercial airplane or vice versa. However, some technicalities make this much more challenging than if you were to do private first in the respective aircraft category (rotorcraft or airplane).

Scenario 1

Remember, the guiding principle behind this scenario is that you will reach the 250 total flight hours before being prepared to take *all* the remaining check rides once you are eligible to take the commercial check ride. Therefore, the order in which you progress through the licenses matters. You want to set yourself up to get the greatest reward for each stopping point. Because of this, I will provide the order that is the simplest and focuses on getting paid sooner rather than later.

The first step is to complete private and instrument. Then, prepare for the single-engine commercial check ride by studying the necessary material, completing the flight requirements, and gaining proficiency in the required maneuvers. Once fully prepared to take the single-engine commercial check ride, minus the required 250 total hours, press pause on your progression with single-engine commercial and turn your focus to CFI. Complete the same tasks in preparation for the CFI check ride. Then, do the same for CFII.

CFI and CFII will have the same maneuvers you did in private, commercial, and instrument. The only difference is you will sit in the right seat instead of the left, which takes time and practice to get used to.

Much of the preparation for CFI and CFII is ground knowledge. Thankfully, this does not eat into the 250 hours of flight time required for commercial, but it will still take a significant amount of time overall. Therefore, you may need more time to prepare for the CFI and CFII check rides while building the flight time to become eligible for the single-engine commercial check ride. That's okay.

The goal here is to knock out as many of the requirements and become prepared for as many check rides as possible with the hours you know you have to pay for any way to save you as much money as possible.

While working on CFI and/or CFII check rides, and you get within roughly ten or so hours of the 250 total flight hours required for commercial, stop working on CFI and CFII to focus solely on the single-engine commercial check ride. Use the remaining time to ensure you are comfortable and proficient with the maneuvers from the left seat to take and pass the check ride.

If you have properly prepared, after you pass the single-engine commercial check ride, you can turn around and take the CFI check ride the same or the next day, followed by CFII.

If you need more flight time or time in general to

prepare for CFI and/or CFII, no worries. Take the necessary time to prepare for them. However, if you are on top of everything and feeling ready for CFI and CFII, there are no legal restrictions preventing you from taking those check rides back to back after the single-engine commercial check ride.

This route keeps you in a single-engine airplane throughout the 250 flight hours and maintains continuity in your progression. This, in turn, helps compartmentalize each license better than if you were bouncing between single-engine and multi-engine airplanes. It also puts you into a position where you can get paid to fly sooner as the licenses you will either finish first, or finish soonest if you need more time, will be instructor licenses.

Once you have obtained CFI, you can start getting paid to fly. Having CFII will create more opportunities to get paid to fly as you open up the ability to teach instrument and CFII instead of only private, commercial, and CFI.

So what happens if you prepare for single-engine commercial, CFI, and CFII, and you still have plenty of hours remaining before hitting the 250? In this case, I recommend completing multi-engine private from start to finish.

Yes, you can skip this license and go straight to multi-engine commercial. However, there are pros and cons to doing this.

Pros

1. You can build up more multi-engine PIC (pilot in command) time. While I do not cover the details of PIC in this book, the biggest draw to PIC time is to help build your resume, especially with those first few jobs outside of flight instructing. It also helps with ATP.

2. You complete the license, which gets it out of the way without having to revisit it like you will with commercial, CFI, and CFII.

3. Your initial intro with multi-engine airplanes will be at the private standards instead of commercial, which provides more of a baby step and should make multi-engine commercial that much easier.

Cons

1. It generally takes more flight hours to obtain both multi-engine private and commercial than it would if you were to go straight for multi-engine commercial.

If you still have enough hours after completing multi-engine private, prepare for multi-engine commercial and then multi-engine instructor (MEI).

Let's recap where you would be at this point. You would be completely done with single-engine private, instrument, and multi-engine private, and you would be prepared for the single and multi-engine commercial, CFI, CFII, and MEI check rides. In other words, you would be done with three check rides and be prepared to take five more back to back.

As you can imagine, that is a lot of information to keep straight and compartmentalized as you progress. It would also take staying up to speed on your ground knowledge with each license and most likely some refresher flights before taking each check ride. As such, this is not for the faint of heart, but it is doable.

Remember, you can stop at any point in this progression as you approach the 250 total flight hours to focus on the single-engine commercial check ride. However, if you have additional remaining flight hours, you want to continue progressing using that time efficiently to prepare for as many of the check rides as possible.

The last thing you need to be aware of is that some check rides must be taken in a specific order. Having an airplane commercial license is a prerequisite to taking any of the airplane instructor check rides, and having CFI is a prerequisite to taking the CFII or MEI check rides. Therefore, you will not be able to take any of these check rides you are now prepared for until you first reach the 250 total flight hours and take one of the commercial check rides (single or multi-engine commercial) first. Despite that, you can still take the check rides in multiple orders. Here are some examples.

1. Single-engine commercial, CFI, CFII, multi-engine commercial, and MEI
2. Single or multi-engine commercial first followed by the other, and then CFI, CFII, and MEI
3. Multi-engine commercial, CFI, CFII, MEI, and then single-engine commercial

The order in which you take these check rides does not matter in the grand scheme of things aside from meeting the prerequisites. Nevertheless, for simplicity and continuity, I recommend doing all the check rides requiring a single-engine airplane first and then those requiring a multi-engine second.

Here are some additional notes you will want to consider.

1. You can take the CFI and CFII check rides in either a single or a multi-engine airplane. However, single-engine airplanes generally cost less to rent per hour.
2. The DPE can only test you on equipment that is inside the aircraft you test in. So if you have two

engines on your airplane instead of one, that opens up more items the DPE can test you on.

3. All multi-engine licenses (multi-engine private, multi-engine commercial, and MEI) must be completed in a multi-engine airplane.

Scenario 2

As a reminder, this scenario is where you know you will get through the requirements and gain the proficiency needed to pass *all* remaining check rides *before* obtaining 250 total flight hours. This would be the epitome of efficiency. It is also the least likely to happen, but it is good to be aware of if you find yourself in a position to do this.

You will first need to complete single-engine private and then instrument. From there, the order in which you progress through the licenses will ultimately be up to you. However, I recommend preparing for them in any of the following orders.

1. Single-engine commercial, CFI, CFII, multi-engine private or straight to multi-engine commercial, MEI
2. Single-engine commercial, multi-engine private or straight to multi-engine commercial, CFI, CFII, MEI
3. Multi-engine private, single-engine commercial, CFI, CFII, multi-engine commercial, MEI
4. Multi-engine private, multi-engine commercial, single-engine commercial, CFI, CFII, MEI

Remember, except for multi-engine private, you will only be able to take these check rides once you have reached the 250 total flight hours for eligibility and have first taken one of the commercial check rides. You must acquire an airplane commercial license before taking the CFI and CFII check rides, and you must have multi-engine commercial before taking the MEI check ride.

As you can see, with these two scenarios, the airplane pilots have a little more to think about and many more options.

For both scenarios, please remember that not everyone will be able to do this. It is simply the most efficient use of your flight time.

If it takes you more than 250 total flight hours to be ready for all your check rides, it does not mean you have failed by any means. It only means you will pay for additional hours beyond the 250 required for commercial, and there is nothing wrong with that. 250 hours is simply the minimum hours you must pay for.

The more prepared you are for multi-engine private and/or multi-engine commercial, CFI, CFII, and MEI before reaching the 250 hours, the fewer total hours you will need to pay for and the more money you will save overall.

If you decide to pursue this route of working ahead of the license you initially started, ensure you continue to study and review the commercial ground knowledge as you are working on the other licenses and building your total time.

Please remember, the priority goal is to ensure you are prepared for and ready to pass whichever commercial check ride you initially start with BEFORE working on any other license.

There is no point in trying to get ahead if you are not in a position to pass the commercial check ride, as commercial is the first gate you must pass.

Take it one license at a time if you need to, but if you can appropriately prepare for the commercial check ride, understand what I am teaching you here, and you are feeling good about it, have at it!

ALL PILOTS

I hope your head isn't swimming right now, as I have one more noteworthy item to discuss that adds to all this.

If you manage to progress and use your flight time such that you have made it through all the licenses and you still have not reached the 150 or 250 hours respectively, there is one last area you can apply the remaining flight time to help yourself out down the road. That is building up the proper flight time for ATP requirements. Specifically, use any remaining time you do not need for the other licenses to build up your night, instrument, and cross-country flight times. I promise you that you will thank yourself later.

SUMMARY

You now know you must be both eligible and proficient to take and pass a check ride. Getting the requirements completed first (aside from the total time requirement) and then working on proficiency will give you the most leeway for getting in those last-minute proficiency flights before a check ride or rescheduling your check ride if needed. Doing so reduces stress by knowing you have met the requirements, which leaves the remaining time for you to work on what you want to work on and will allow you to get ahead in your training. Using your flight time wisely will maximize each flight hour and dollar you spend.

10

PROGRESSING THROUGH TRAINING EFFICIENTLY
PART 2
KNOWLEDGE

There is a substantial amount of information you will learn throughout flight training. By the time you finish this book, you will know how to find and list out all the flight requirements and be aware of all the books you will need to read for each license. Once you have those, you will be able to see percentage-wise how far along you are with both.

Flying and studying go hand in hand. Flying supplements the knowledge, and knowledge supplements the flying. You need both to maximize your learning.

Imagine trying to build a car for the first time where you have all the parts and a very detailed manual of how to put it all together.

If you read the entire manual before ever putting your hands on the car, you would have to go back and reread a lot of the information as you attempted to assemble the car from memory. Similarly, suppose you were to immediately start working on the car without ever reading the manual. In that case, you may be able to assemble a good chunk of the car, but you would probably make plenty of mistakes along the way and take longer to complete it as you redo much of the work.

The most efficient way to assemble the car would be to read a little, work a little, and repeat until the car is complete. Doing both simultaneously would be more efficient than doing one or the other in its entirety and then the other.

The same principle applies to flight school. If you only read first or only fly first and then do the other, you would progress slower than you would if you progressed in both simultaneously.

A general rule of thumb is <u>for every hour of flying, do two or more hours of studying</u>. This way, your studying will stay up to par with your flying. For most, it is easier to progress faster in flying than with ground knowledge. Be aware of this and control the rate you progress in your flying compared to your knowledge.

The goal is to progress through the flying and knowledge at roughly the same rate. For example, when you are halfway through the flight requirements, you should be at least halfway done with the reading and ground knowledge.

With that said, being further along in your reading and studying is acceptable and preferred, but only to an extent, because it is generally quicker and easier to catch up with your flying skills than your knowledge level.

Getting behind on reading and studying is where most problems and frustrations arise. Usually, students do not process the reality of this problem until they are ready to take the flying portion of the check ride but are not even close to being prepared for the oral portion or have failed to take their knowledge test.

In this case, most students stop flying altogether to spend the time to bring their studying up to par and/or take the knowledge test. This delay can take a couple of days or up to months. All while not flying.

What do you think happens to your handling skills of the aircraft during the time it takes to do this? What about your motivation? How many flight hours will it take to regain that proficiency and confidence?

Depending on how long you don't fly and how quickly you become proficient again will determine how many flight hours it will take for you to get caught back up to be ready for both the oral and the flight portions of the check ride.

I already talked in detail about being efficient with your flight time. This is not the way to do it.

It is essential to pay attention to your overall progression in both flying and knowledge. You can use the Part 61/141 checklists you will learn about later to help keep this balance.

If you notice your knowledge starting to fall behind, slow down or take a break from flying until your knowledge catches back up. It is better to slow down the flying in the middle of the training than just before a check ride, as you want as much recency in the aircraft right before each check ride as possible.

Overall, for time and cost efficiency, keep the knowledge portion progressing equal to or greater than the flying as you implement your plans of action for each flight, focus on checking off all the flight requirements first, and then polish up your proficiency on maneuvers second.

11

STAYING FOCUSED ON WHAT
MATTERS MOST

PRIORITIES

Here comes another analogy. Bear with me. Imagine multiple large, fenced-in fields lined up next to the other in a row full of tall, luscious, green grass. Each field is separated from the other by gates lined up throughout the center of each field.

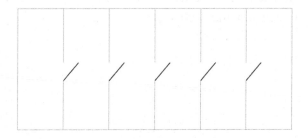

Now imagine you are a hungry cow (my spirit animal), and you are standing against the fence on the far side of the first field. The most distant field from you has the greenest grass, oats, alfalfa, and whatever else a cow loves to eat. As such, that last field is where you ultimately want to go.

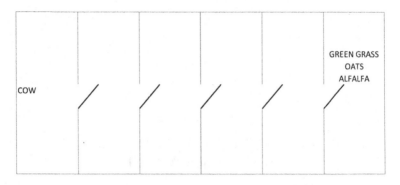

To get to that last field, you must cross the first field, pass through the narrow gate into the following field, cross that field, get through its gate, and so on.

Here is the catch. The only way you can move through the field is to eat yourself a path through the delicious green grass. This leaves you with two primary options as you cross each field.

You can wander around each field eating all the tasty grass your three-stomach body desires while taking your sweet time and eventually getting to each gate. Or, you can take the quickest, shortest, least grass-you-have-to-eat way to get to the last field with the greenest grass, which is a straight line between you and each gate.

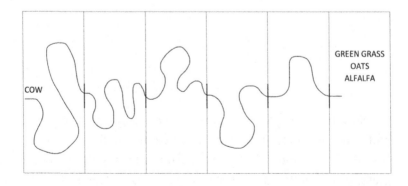

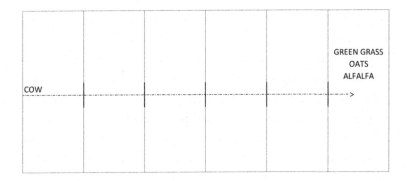

In this analogy, the fields represent each license you will get, with the last field representing finishing flight school. The gates in this analogy are your upcoming check rides. The delicious grass is the endless quantity of books and resources containing beneficial information you would like to know as a pilot that is not required but may still help you get through the gate. The straight path between you and the gate represents the minimum requirements and knowledge necessary to take and pass your check ride. The squiggly line is the inefficient, time-consuming path. Lastly, my guidance in this book will serve as a visible line in the grass to help keep you on that straight path.

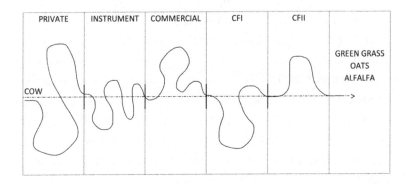

While this may be a quirky analogy, it helps picture a

scenario students often find themselves in when working on a check ride.

Looking at the squiggly line through each field seems comical. You may be thinking, "Why would anyone do that? Obviously, that is not the way to go." However, in the reality of life, it is easy to get distracted by things that do not matter in the moment and will not help move the needle forward. This, in turn, eats up your time and delays you from reaching your goals.

The crazy part is it is hard to recognize the path you are taking at the moment, but it is easy to see where you got off course when you look back at the end. Recognize that this happens and use it to focus on what matters most at the moment. Doing so will help you achieve your goals in the shortest time possible.

I did fail to mention in my analogy the inevitable cow-pies lying around in the field from previous cows. While cow pies can be beneficial in helping fertilize the field to create more delicious grass to feed other cows (valuable knowledge and information that will help propel you along that straight line), it takes time for a cow pie to go through its full process to be beneficial instead of a nuisance. These lovely cow pies are representative of study groups.

Depending on how knowledgeable and focused those participating in the study group are determines how beneficial or not the study group is.

A hot and fresh cow pie would be students disseminating incorrect and/or incomplete information or wasting time chatting about non-aviation related topics. A fertilizing cow pie helping to create more luscious green grass would be students that know the correct information, where to find it, and stay on topic. More on this later.

Unless you have an incredibly determined flight instructor who pushes you along, no one is holding your hoof in the field, and you are free to take as much time as you want to roam around eating all the grass you would like.

Remember, the faster you get through each gate and reach that last field, the sooner you start getting paid to fly. And, once you reach that farthest field, you can freely go back into the other fields whenever you want to partake of all the delicious grass your large cow heart desires when you are not on a time crunch. How is that for some food for thought?

KNOWING THE RIGHT ANSWERS

I will let you in on something that is not a secret, but for how few people seem to process this next part, it may as well be one.

The FAA came up with the requirements you need to meet to get your licenses. The FAA provides all the information you will get tested on for free. And the FAA tests you by looking for answers from the information they specifically disseminate.

In other words, the FAA came up with the game, defined the rules, and will evaluate you on everything they came up with based on their rules. If this is the case and you are looking for the most efficient way to get your licenses, why would you pay to obtain and spend valuable time reading any other material not required and not put out by the FAA? The answer is you don't need to, and if time is of the essence, you shouldn't.

Just as the grass is delicious in the analogy, the information put out by other various companies and sources is, for the most part, fantastic and beneficial information that can help you pass your check rides.

These different sources generally present the information in a much cleaner, more precise, and more organized manner than what the FAA provides. After all, the FAA is a faction of the government, and we all know the government is not always the best at delivering precise, easy-to-understand information (#IRS).

However, you must pay for these other books, and you can run into the following potential issue.

If there is a difference in information, no matter how small, between what the FAA disseminates and these other sources, guess which source of information will provide the correct answer on check ride day. You got it, the FAA's, since the FAA is testing you on their information.

How will you know if there is a difference between the same topic put out by the FAA and the others? You won't unless you have read both stances on the information. And if you have already read the FAA's view on it, why would you spend your time reading the others when you could be using that same time to read and study the bountiful FAA sources of information you still need to learn and know to pass the check ride?

Again, the point of this book is to teach you how to complete flight training in the most efficient manner possible regarding time and money. The most efficient way to learn the necessary knowledge is to only read what is required and read it directly from the source. Doing so will give you complete, accurate information and will help you learn where to reference it later.

Nevertheless, if you want to read the other sources or additional information, go for it. There is no harm in gaining further knowledge. It will only take more time, which decreases efficiency.

Another way to think about this is this. Let's say you need to put in 1,000 hours of dedicated studying to finish flight school, and you have a master clock counting down the 1,000 hours by the minute. The moment that last minute lapses, flight school would be complete and not a second earlier. The only way the clock counts down is when you are 100% mentally dedicated to studying. If you knew the only way to finish flight school was to put in the 1,000 hours of studying, wouldn't you be more inclined to dedicate the time to studying?

While this analogy is more clear-cut and provides a great visual aid for progression, flight school works the same way. Instead of a clock counting down, you have a set number of requirements to meet and a baseline knowledge you must obtain. The only way to progress through either of those is to dedicate time to studying and working through them. No one else can do that for you. It must be you. The more distractions you have, the longer it will take, so remove the distractions and use your time wisely.

As I have discussed, there are more efficient study methods than others. The more efficient your studying, the quicker you progress and the sooner you can get paid to fly.

Therefore, keep your head down, put in the work, keep your eye on the prize, and step by step, you will cross that field, pass through the gate, and repeat until you are standing in the last field.

After you have passed through all the gates, please, please, please go back and eat all the other grass you can at that point by reading anything and everything you can get your hands on related to aviation. Doing so will make you a safer and more competent pilot and flight instructor.

12

THE RIGHT MENTALITY AND LEARNING TO TEACH

A pproach flight school with the mentality that you will become a flight instructor and teach everything you are learning to new pilots who will be standing where you are today.

Even though there is no requirement to become a flight instructor, and not all pilots become one, approaching flight school with the mentality that you will become an instructor will only benefit you.

This mindset will propel you on the right path to help you learn everything the right way the first time with greater detail and a better understanding. Whether you become an instructor or not, this approach to studying will make you a safer, more knowledgeable, and more competent pilot.

Let's revisit the two groups of licenses I discussed in Chapter 7. If you recall, with two small exceptions, the only difference between the information contained within each group is the required level of comprehension.

It was also determined once you get to the instructor license in each group, you will be teaching the information found in the previous licenses for their respective group.

GROUP 1	GROUP 2
Private	Instrument
Commercial	CFII
CFI	

This being the case, why not strive to learn each topic well enough you can teach it the first time through? In other words, why not learn the subjects taught in private well enough to teach them at the CFI level while working on private? Or learn the topics taught in instrument well enough to teach them at the CFII level while working on instrument?

The only requirement to teach something is under-standing it well enough to regurgitate it. Let me explain.

Teaching may sound daunting initially, but it is easier than it may seem, especially with some practice. All you need to do is read something, understand it well enough to put it into your own words, and then regurgitate it.

You already do this with your family and friends when-ever you tell a story about something that has happened in your life. Instead of reading about it, the events unfolded in front of you, you recall the events in your mind, and then you put them into your own words as you regurgitate the story. You may not recount all the details perfectly, but you get the point across.

Sometimes, the story gets told better and more completely than others, and generally, the more you tell the story, the better it gets.

The only difference between telling that story and teaching an aviation concept is how you perceive the actions and what the information is about. If you think about it, they are both stories you are telling, and that is all there is to it. Study with the attitude that teaching is easy, and it will be. So, start with the mentality that you are learning to teach, not just understand.

Here is a prime example of why you can and should apply this process. You will read through the Pilot's Handbook of Aeronautical Knowledge (PHAK) when going through private. You will reread it for commercial and again for CFI. Do you think the information contained in the book changes each time? Nope. It is the same book and the same information.

The only difference is you pick up on more details each time you read it because you will have more experience than the time prior and be able to absorb more information, like watching a movie. The more you watch the same movie, the more details you pick up.

However, you can still get everything, or at least as much as possible, out of the PHAK the first time you read it while in private. And as you now know, it only takes understanding the concept to teach it.

If you cannot logically talk through the topic, then you do not understand the information well enough. Reread the subject and work through it. Sure, it takes a little more time than just reading the words on a page, but you need to know the information anyway to pass each check ride, so why not spend a little extra time to ensure you understand it the first time through?

Another point to address is you can still use the references when you teach. The material you teach does not all have to be memorized. Nevertheless, the better you understand a topic, the more you will naturally remember and the easier it will be to teach.

Think of it this way. The first time you learned how to bake a cake, you followed a recipe. If you were to turn around and teach someone else how to bake the same cake, you would remember most of the steps and ingredients you need. However, you may have to reference the recipe for the quantity of each ingredient and the temperature to cook it.

Teaching piloting is the same way. You need to know the bulk of the subject but can reference the material when needed for the details. The more you know without looking things up, the better, but the references are there if or when you need them.

Here is how to apply this. Once you finish reading about a topic, take a few minutes to talk through it *out loud* in your own words.

For example, if you just read up on Bernoulli's Principle and it made sense as you were reading, set the book down and try to explain it in your own words out loud to yourself. If you sound like a three-year-old recounting their day where the words are mostly correct, but the order and sequence of events are like a pinball bouncing all over the place, reread the topic and try again. Repeat the process until you can talk yourself through the entire topic from start to finish, having it make sense and including all the details.

The goal is to adequately explain the topic to someone who knows nothing about it and have them follow and understand you without asking too many follow-up questions.

The better you understand the topic and the more you rehearse the information, the easier it will become to teach, and you will incidentally begin to commit it all to memory.

Here is a tip to help as you practice explaining topics to yourself and teaching others.

Imagine the topic you are teaching is the picture of a puzzle, and the details of that topic are the puzzle pieces. You know what the picture looks like because you already know the topic you are about to teach. However, the person you are teaching does not.

Because of this, imagine that you are starting with a blank puzzle. It is up to you to paint the whole picture correctly, piece by piece, and ensure that each piece fits together in the end to form the complete picture properly.

Begin with an overview of the entire picture so whoever you are teaching has an idea of what to expect, and then break it down piece by piece in an order that makes sense and will ensure all the pieces properly fit together.

Remember that everything you say is the equivalent of painting something onto one of the puzzle pieces. Each mistake you make with incorrect or misplaced information is the same as a wrong or missed brush stroke, which skews the puzzle piece and, consequently, the overall picture.

Skipping over details would be the same as missing pieces of the puzzle, and improperly explaining how things come together would be the equivalent of incorrectly assembling the puzzle. Doing these things, or leaving them as they are, will cause the picture to look cluttered and chaotic, just like the three-year-old recounting the events of their day. The person you are teaching may still understand the gist of the big picture, but they will ask more follow-up questions than if they had seen the picture as was intended.

If you feel you can explain the whole puzzle to yourself and the picture looks right, then try teaching it to a friend or significant other. Their reactions and any follow-up questions they ask will let you know how well you did and whether you need to explain it differently. You will know if you are on track when you can explain the topic such that there are no follow-up questions and the individual you taught truly understands the topic.

Taking the time to do this the first time you read each new topic will take longer on the front end but will save you an incredible amount of time on the back end. While you do not have to do this with every topic you read about, strive to do it with the more complex subjects that build on themselves such as principles of lift and others.

Keep in mind, the better you understand the information

yourself the better you will be able to teach it. Some topics will take more practice than others.

Approaching your studying this way will ensure you understand each concept, are more likely to remember it, and you will be better prepared to teach it if or when you become an instructor.

Remember, even if you do not plan on becoming an instructor, being able to teach each topic as if you were will help you understand the concept that much better making you a more competent and safer pilot.

The speaking-out-loud part throughout this process is incredibly important as well. Vocalizing everything helps both on the ground and in the air and has different benefits for each.

By vocalizing the topics on the ground, you will recognize whether your ideas and words flow and make sense, and if you are properly painting the picture, helps you remember the information, get used to hearing your voice in a teaching capacity, and build confidence in speaking in front of others.

Vocalizing everything you are doing in the aircraft is a little different than vocalizing things on the ground as there is a lot more going on in the aircraft and your voice sounds different which has a greater effect than you may realize. Vocalizing everything you are doing in the aircraft will:

1. help you process what it is you are doing
2. help you catch your mistakes by recognizing the difference between what you are saying the aircraft should be doing compared to what the aircraft is doing
3. let your instructor know what you are thinking so they know if you are doing things intentionally or not and if they need to intervene

4. let the DPE know during a check ride whether you have recognized a mistake and if you are going to correct it, which often buys you a little more leeway if you are right on the cusp of failing
5. help you prepare to become an instructor by making you more comfortable hearing the sound of your voice in the aircraft through the headset
6. allow you to become more efficient at teaching and talking through each maneuver as you fly the aircraft
7. help you recognize the timing of when to speak and when to listen to the radios and other people in the aircraft
8. increase your situational awareness as you multitask in the aircraft

The more you talk through topics on the ground and in the air, the more efficiently and effectively you can teach. You will find better ways to explain concepts and ideas, and you will find any gaps in your knowledge as the people you teach ask you follow-up questions.

You will learn way more teaching than you ever will just by reading and learning the information as you go through flight school.

Remember, this is a learning process. No pilot was born knowing everything. All pilots had to start where you are now. If you begin your training with the expectation to teach everything, you will progress much faster and be a more well-rounded pilot.

Whether you become an instructor or not, your goal as a pilot should be to hear a topic and be able to teach everything there is about it. You will not necessarily be able to do this while working on private, but the more you strive for this early on, the more you will learn, and the rest of your training will be easier because of the good habits you will develop.

Just as I have taught you to anticipate teaching everything you will learn, you should also look ahead to find and hold yourself to the strictest standards you will eventually be required to perform each flight maneuver to. It will be challenging initially, but your aircraft handling will progress faster doing this. And, since you will have to get there eventually, you might as well find the most restrictive standards upfront, use them as your baseline, and accept nothing less.

Just like everything else, holding yourself to the highest standard now will only make each lower standard that much easier to meet, especially when it comes to flying. As they say in the movie The Patriot, "Aim small, miss small."

13

HOW TO APPROACH STUDYING

You need to know the following three things each time you start working on a new license.

The first is knowing which books and resources you need to read. I will provide a condensed priority list of what you need to read and teach you how to find the complete list in a later chapter.

Second, you actually need to read each of the books. Sounds crazy, I know, but the information must get in your head somehow, and this is by far the cheapest and fastest way to get it there. Plus, reading the books yourself ensures you get complete, accurate information directly from the source and helps with the third thing.

Third, you need to know the general information in each book so you can quickly look things up. Initially, you can do this by reading through the table of contents at the front of the book or going through the index in the back, if there is one, to find a specific topic and the associated page number. Once you have read through each book, you will be more familiar with the contents in each and will be able to look items up that much quicker.

Many topics in flight school build off each other, similar to math. You need to know the basic principle before you move on to the next. Because of this, you need to understand what you are reading as you go.

If what you read does not make sense, read it again. If it still does not make sense, do an online search, ask your friends or classmates, and if you still need help understanding the concept, write it down and ask an available instructor at the hangar. All of which are free sources of information.

If you are still unclear about what you are studying, set up a ground lesson with your instructor where you will pay them to clarify the concepts you need help understanding. Don't let your questions go unanswered, and do not be afraid to ask questions. An unanswered question often leads to further confusion or lack of understanding down the road that builds off what you were initially unsure of. Remove the stumbling block sooner rather than later so it does not become a boulder to overcome.

READ, DISCUSS, IMPLEMENT

To better learn, understand, and memorize new information, utilize the read, discuss, and implement process to each new concept.

First, read the information from the source for complete, accurate information and know where to reference it (you have heard this a few times now, so it must be important). Doing so allows the law of primacy (what you learn first sticks best) to work in your favor. Plus, you can read at your own pace in a distraction-free area where you can pause, think, and reread as many times as you need to understand the information better.

Next, discuss it. Discussing the information after reading

it helps ensure understanding and solidifies the knowledge in your head.

The more you talk about or hear the information, the more you will understand and remember it.

If you have a classroom setting where you know what you will be talking about the next day, read the information beforehand and write down any questions you come up with. This way, you will go into class with a baseline knowledge and hear it a second time when it is taught. This helps to solidify the knowledge. Additionally, you may get your questions answered in the process. If they still need to get answered, ask for clarification. Chances are, if you have a question, others will have the same question. Write down the answers you receive to reference later.

If you do not have a classroom setting, discuss the information with fellow pilots in training, pester your significant other, or talk through it out loud by yourself, as previously mentioned. The idea is to go over the information more than once to get confirmation that you learned the topic correctly, understand it, and have it stick in your head. Ideally, this happens while interacting with someone else as that adds another set of eyes and ears to confirm what you know or correct you if need be.

Lastly, implement it. Do this by taking what you have learned into the air and trying it out during a flight, if applicable. Or, teach the concept to someone else and see if they understand it. If they cannot follow you as you teach it, do not understand it, or ask too many follow-up questions, work on how you present the information and try again. Remember, you are painting a picture for someone using puzzle pieces, and practice makes perfect.

SELF-SUFFICIENCY

As you go about your day in and out of the hangar, you will hear new topics and acronyms you are unfamiliar with, think of random questions, and strive to remember various principles and ideas you may have forgotten. All of which can be resolved by quickly looking up the answer.

Just as when you study, write these questions down if you cannot look them up right away. Doing so will help you to remember to look them up the first chance you get. You will eventually need the answers to these questions, so get them answered sooner rather than later.

Try to be as self-sufficient as possible in finding answers by looking these questions up yourself. Use whichever book you think would have the answer, skim through the table of contents or the index for the most relatable topic to your question, and then read through the associated pages.

Self-reliance is the goal.

Once you are an instructor or working a pilot job beyond the scope of flight training, *you* will be your primary source of information. Knowing the correct answer is important, but knowing how to find the correct answer creates independence.

If you have ever heard the saying by Chinese philosopher Lao Tzu, "Give a man a fish and you feed him for a day. Teach him how to fish and you feed him for a lifetime," this is where that comes into play. Nevertheless, if you legitimately cannot find the answers to your questions on your own, do not be afraid to reach out for help. To save money, utilize the free resources first before paying for ground.

STUDY GROUPS

You will encounter plenty of flight students who want to get together to do study groups. As previously discussed, these can be extremely helpful if you use them at the right time and for the right reasons.

I have been to plenty of study groups as a student, an instructor, and again later in my career. They can be a lot of fun. You get to meet new people, get to know people better, and chat about all sorts of things both related to aviation and not. All good stuff, but if getting through flight training as quickly as possible is your goal, as I mentioned before, study groups are not the way, especially at the start of a new license. Use that time to read and study the things you need to know and work on.

The biggest problem with study groups is when the discussion turns toward something you have yet to read about. There is no way for you to know if the information is complete and accurate unless someone reads it directly from the book. And, if they are reading directly from the book, you may as well be doing that by yourself at your own pace without distractions.

I cannot count the number of times people in study groups would start a sentence with, "I heard it was this way" or "My instructor said this." If you notice, neither is, "This is what the book says."

These are prime examples of people not going straight to the source, reading the book, and knowing the correct information for themselves. It is all word of mouth, which is the same as playing the game Telephone, where one person starts by whispering a sentence into the ear of the person next to them, who then whispers the same sentence to the next person, and so on.

By the time it gets to the end, the bulk of the sentence may be correct, but small words and details may have changed. These differences can alter the intent and meaning of the sentence.

This process happens frequently in study groups and is a complete disservice to everyone involved. Again, aim for efficiency. Speed and accuracy are everything.

I am not telling you to avoid socializing and hanging out with other friends in training. There will be plenty of times you will want to take a break from the intense studying to socialize with like-minded people and friends. That is great. Nurture and build your network, but realize there is a difference between getting together to hang out and getting together as a study group with the intent to learn. Know the difference and know when to do each.

The best use of a proper study group for your gain is when you have already read the information, have a baseline understanding of it, know where to find it, and all you need is some clarification. Because of this, it is more efficient to avoid the study groups until you have read the books.

Once you have read the books and know the information reasonably well, then participate in the study groups. Be the one to help the others. Lead the discussion and teach the group what you know. Then, any time someone says they heard something is this way or that, or this is what so and so said, you can easily correct them. Or, if needs be, you can quickly look up the answer in the book to show them the proper source and correct answer.

By leading the study group, you will have more chances to teach. Teaching helps you understand the information better, discover more ways to teach the topics, and helps you to remember the information.

❧ 14 ❧

FAA.GOV

Faa.gov is an invaluable website where you can get all the references and publications you will need to read for free.

Each time I have mentioned reading from the source, this is ultimately it. Faa.gov is also where you find the most up-to-date version of everything sourced by the FAA. You can even download and print PDFs of each book if you want access to them offline.

The layout of the website changes periodically, so any details of the layout and location of information on the website would be futile. As long as you can find the search bar within the website, you will be good to go.

Pro-tip with the search bar. You may need to search for the acronym of what you are looking for, spell it all out, or sometimes you need to use keywords. It is hit-and-miss, so if you do not find what you are looking for the first time, change the format of your search words and try again. Then, scan through the links that come up and click on the most applicable link.

On rare occasions, you may need to navigate through the

links found on the homepage of faa.gov to find what it is you are looking for. If you don't specifically know what you are looking for, do a general search online and use the results with links to faa.gov. Then, once you follow the link, ensure you have the current edition of whatever reference you are looking up.

Or, if you are looking for a regulation, do a general online search for "What regulation talks about [insert your topic]." One of the results is bound to have the regulation number in the preview line. Instead of following that link, use the reg number to lookup the regulation within faa.gov.

The FAA offers the ability to look at historical regulations and current regulations. Verify you are in the current regulations each time you look up a reg. It is hard enough to memorize all the numbers and regs as it is. You do not want to make life any more complicated by muddying the waters with outdated information.

THE ACS

I f you stop to think about it for a moment, you now know many things that you do not know. Sounds contradictory, I know. But here is what I mean is this. You now know that you must pass a written test, an oral evaluation, and a flight evaluation to get your first license. Yet you do not know the information necessary to pass those tests. You know what you do not know. Or, in other words, you are aware of what you do not know.

Knowing what you do not know is the first and most important step to taking charge of your flight training or anything else in life, and it prevents you from waiting around wondering what the next step is.

Knowing what you do not know allows you to take the initiative to learn what you do not know, which, in turn, keeps your learning progressing to obtain your goal. It enables you to control the pace of your learning, what you learn, when, and how to best utilize your instructor, instead of your instructor telling you what to learn, when, and at what pace.

Another analogy to better picture this is creating the framework for your house of knowledge. You need the framework first to identify the confines and limits of what you are working with so you can appropriately fill in the rest of the house. The framework is being aware of what you do not know, and the rest of the house comes with learning those things.

The framework for flight school knowledge comes in the form of a book called the Airman Certification Standards (ACS) or the Practical Test Standards (PTS), depending on which aircraft category you are flying. The ACS or PTS will list all the things you need to know for each license, allowing you to become aware of what you do not know. Then, it is up to you to learn those things.

The ACS is simply a newer version of the PTS, and the PTS is getting phased out. Therefore, by the time you read this, all licenses, whether rotorcraft or airplane, may be utilizing the ACS. However, as of writing this, all airplane licenses, except CFI and CFII, are using the ACS, and rotorcraft are utilizing the PTS.

The purpose of changing to the ACS is to make the testing process more scenario-based. This requires the applicant to have a better working understanding of the information they learn instead of rote memorization. The layout and order of the information are also different.

Aside from those minor nuances, the ACS and PTS are basically the same. Because of this, the term ACS in this book will refer to both ACS and PTS unless specified otherwise.

The ACS is the answer key to your check ride. More specifically, it contains a comprehensive list of all the resources you need to read through that cover everything you can be tested on for each check ride. There are appendixes that cover additional information you will need to know as well.

The appendixes cover areas such as what equipment you must use for the check ride, what the DPE is required to test you on, what parts are optional (if any), what happens if you fail or need to discontinue, and many other noteworthy items you will want to be aware of, and need to know, including information about knowledge tests.

There are multiple published ACS books. Each one covers a specific license. However, some ACS books cover more than one license within the same book. They are intuitive, and as long as you match up the title of the specific ACS with the license you are working on, you will be good to go.

The FAA publishes the various ACS books, which are available for free on faa.gov. So yes, all the questions to each check ride are posted and made readily available for free whenever you want to look at them. Just go to faa.gov, search "Certification Standards," find the appropriate link that lists out all the ACS books, and look for the license you are seeking within that link. This applies to both the ACS and PTS.

If a teacher at school gave you a sheet with all the questions to the test before you had to take it, would you not want to look through the questions and find as many of the answers as possible beforehand? That is precisely what the FAA has done here. Plus, the ACS is a quick read!

You should read it cover to cover at least once to familiarize yourself with everything in there. From there, you will refer to it from time to time to see what you need to study.

The ACS lists categories that have been broken down into smaller subjects in an organized manner. These subjects start at preflight and work their way through postflight and pertain to the license you are seeking.

Before taking each check ride, you should use the ACS as a checklist to verify you know everything you are supposed to. The ACS lists everything you need to know in a format similar to a PowerPoint presentation, where you see the key ideas you need to discuss without having all the details written out. If you can go through each line item and confidently explain and expound on each topic, you will know you are ready for the oral portion of the check ride.

The ACS also lists all the flight maneuvers you will perform and to what standard. An example would be to roll out of your turns within ±10° of a specified heading, level off ±100' of a predetermined altitude, and maintain a set speed of ±10 knots. Again, look through the ACS books for all the licenses you will end up with to find the most restrictive standards for each maneuver upfront, and then hold yourself to those standards right out of the gate.

Each ACS has a page listing every reference used to create that specific ACS. The references page is at the back end of each ACS and closer to the front of each PTS. The FAA generates every one of the references listed throughout the ACS and PTS books and is available for free online at faa.gov.

Each reference listed in the applicable ACS you use is fair game for the DPE to draw questions from and test you on during the oral evaluation. Because of this, the references page in the ACS is the complete mandatory reading list for that license.

Keep in mind that this is a very comprehensive list. Some items are more applicable than others, and while you are required to read through and be familiar with each reference listed, some references are more beneficial than others.

I will not tell you to skip over any of the listed references in the ACS because they are all mandatory, but I will say this. If you are trying to be quick and efficient with your studying and you know you could get 50% of the answers to a test from one reference, 35% from another, and 10% from a third, but then you would need to read ten other books to get the last 5% of the answers you need, which references are you going to read first, prioritize, and spend the most time in? As such, the reading lists I provide later will be the primary references you should read first and prioritize to find most of the answers and information you need. Then, follow up with the remaining references from the references page in the ACS.

The primary takeaway from this chapter is this. Once you know what license you will be working on, read through the applicable ACS before reading anything else.

Reading through and using the ACS as intended will inform you of everything you need to study. You will have a complete list of references to read and everything the DPE can test you on. And, as long as you are honest with yourself, you will also know if and when you are ready to take the oral portion of the check ride. Because of this, there should be no surprises when you go into the check ride.

If you are familiar with all the information in each reference listed in the ACS, you will know everything the DPE can fail you on. This means that the DPE can only fail you for not knowing the answers to questions based on the references listed on the references page in the ACS.

In the rare chance you get a DPE that tries to fail you for not knowing the answer to a question from a reference not listed in the ACS, you can rebuttal the failure.

Another similar potential scenario is getting asked a legitimate question that has two differing answers depending on which reference you get your answer from. If the DPE says the correct answer is from a reference not listed in the ACS and fails you for that specific question, again, you can rebuttal the failure.

Do you recall the scenario where the FAA may have one stance on a particular subject, a third-party reference has a different stance on the same subject, and which stance would be correct? This is where that comes into play.

All answers must come from the references listed in the ACS, and all references in each ACS are made available for free by the FAA on faa.gov.

Remember, the FAA came up with the game, made the rules, and the DPEs who are representatives of the FAA are evaluating you on those rules based on the FAA's information. The path of least resistance comes by playing the FAA's game the way they intended it to be played.

For your awareness, the DPE can ask you all the random questions outside the ACS they want, but they cannot fail you for not knowing the correct answers to those specific questions.

As you can see, the ACS is critically important, which is why it is the very first resource I encourage students to read.

Use the ACS as intended, and it will remove all the guesswork. Read it, and you will know what references you need to read, what you need to know, and the standards you will need to fly each maneuver to. Then, when you feel prepared for the check ride, you can do an accurate self-check by going through each line item in the ACS to know if you are indeed ready.

More importantly, reading through and knowing the ACS inside and out will allow you to take charge of your training by giving you the framework to develop your own plan of action instead of relying on your instructor.

Stress comes from a lack of preparation, and success favors the prepared. Use the ACS to prepare, and you will be prepared to succeed.

🞯 16 🞯

THE FAR/AIM

WHAT IS IT?

F AR stands for Federal Aviation Regulation, and AIM
stands for Aeronautical Information Manual.
Together, they are known as the FAR/AIM.
Pronounced "far aim."

When you hear someone refer to the regs, regulations, FARs, F-A-Rs, or anything along those lines in flight training, they are referring to the FARs.

The FARs are a list of all the federal regulations that apply to aviation and belong to Title 14- Aeronautics and Space, which is one of many titles that help make up the overall United States Code of Federal Regulations (CFRs), which are the laws and regulations of the United States.

The Aeronautical Information Manual is referred to by the AIM, its full name, or occasionally A-I-M.

The AIM provides the rules of the road for how to operate within the National Airspace System (NAS). It acts as a supplement to the FARs that explains some of the regs in layman's terms and provides excellent insight into a variety of topics.

For simplicity, the FARs are like a dictionary that is direct and straight to the point in defining laws with lawyer language. The AIM is more of an encyclopedia that explains principles and concepts in plain English and adds pictures to assist.

Despite being two separate books, in the print version, they are typically combined into one thick book. They are both also available once again for free online at faa.gov. Additionally, you can find FAR/AIM apps. If you decide to go with an app, ensure it pulls its data from faa.gov regularly so that you always have the most up-to-date information.

The print book is convenient for studying. However, the laws can change at any time. Because of this, the books have the potential to be outdated the moment they are finalized and ready to print. Let alone published and distributed to you. If there is a change in the regulations any time after the book is ready to be printed, you will not see the update unless you look online or wait until next year's copy. So, not only do you have to pay for the print version, but it has the potential to be outdated as well.

HOW TO LOOK UP REGULATIONS

You will be in the regulations a lot and not just during flight training. The FARs will likely be the most used reference throughout your aviation career. As such, it is crucial you learn how to look up regulations.

The layout I explain may vary slightly from the source of regulations you are using, but the principles remain the same. The Federal Aviation Regulations are broken down into parts, subparts, sections, and subsections.

The most efficient way to look up regulations in the hard

copy of the FAR/AIM is by using the table of contents at the beginning of the regulations.

The table of contents will list all the parts contained in the book with a brief description of each part. Use the descriptions to figure out the part you are looking for.

Then, close the book and look at the pages from the non-spine side of the book. You will see a few black blocks printed across the side of the pages. These black blocks act as built-in tabs showing the pages that make up each part.

Flip through to find the first page of the part you are looking for. There, you will find another smaller table of contents that lists each subpart and all the regulations listed within the subpart. Each subpart will have a title or brief description of what it discusses. Find the subpart that most applies and then the regulation within that subpart.

The regulation will have an associated number next to it, such as 61.102. The numbers for the different parts and regulations increase sequentially throughout the book.

Summed up, find the part, subpart, section, and subsection or regulation.

If you opt to use an app or the electronic FARs (ECFRs) on faa.gov, the searching process will be much more streamlined because of the layout and hyperlinks, but the process will still ultimately be the same. Find the applicable part, subpart, section, and then subsection or specific reg.

If you are feeling overwhelmed right now on how to do this, don't fret. It sounds much more complicated than it is. Once you have a few minutes to look through the regulations via the book, an app, or online with the ECFRs, it will quickly make sense.

WHICH REGULATIONS TO STUDY

Depending on which method you use to get the regulations (print book, app, or faa.gov), you may have a suggested study list of regulations for each license.

In the past, this list has been placed at the very beginning before you get to any of the regulations. The suggested study list will have the name of each license with a breakout of each applicable part and specific regulations that fall within each part.

Most sources will have the suggested study list, but not all. I have seen the list in the print book by ASA and on ASA's FAR/AIM app.

The suggested study list provides an excellent starting point when you begin studying the regulations and will get you through the majority of the regs you will need to know. However, the list does not necessarily include all the regulations you will need to know for that license. It is simply a great place to start, especially if you are feeling overwhelmed by the number of regulations you need to study and need something smaller and more specific to begin with.

For a complete list of regulations to study, find the references page in the associated ACS. This list will state each part you need to know, which is broad but all-encompassing, as each part has numerous regulations. It does NOT identify the specific regulations within each part.

Therefore, if you were to take it at face value and read each part listed in its entirety, you would read through numerous regulations that clearly do not apply to the flight school realm, such as regulations on large or turbojet aircraft.

As you can see, your options are: 1. Use the suggested study list that breaks out specific regulations within the required parts but only includes *most* of what you are required to know, or 2. You can use the references page in the

ACS that will list all the required *parts* you need to know but does not break out the specific regulations within those parts. Both have their pros and cons.

The moral of the story is that if you feel overwhelmed with the FARs, start with the suggested study list and then use the ACS list to ensure you learn all the regulations you need to know.

Do your best to memorize as many of the FARs as possible as you read through them. The more you have memorized, the better.

Many of the laws are straightforward, but some are rather lengthy and contain many exceptions and limitations. Flash-cards come in handy for the latter.

As you read each regulation, pay close attention to detail. Specifically when you see the words "and" and "or." These small words make a world of difference when complying with regulations.

While you do not necessarily need to memorize each regulation word for word, you need to know the right intent, restrictions, and privileges of each. I am sure you can recognize the hazards associated with misreading and memorizing the wrong intent of a regulation.

Learning the wrong intent of a regulation could be as negligible as answering incorrectly on a check ride or as drastic as having your licenses suspended or revoked, or even potential injury or death. Again, the more regulations you know and have memorized, the easier your check rides will be, the less likely you are to break the law, and the safer you will be.

When you first flip through the FARs, you will see numerous parts. You will not need to know every part during flight school. Initially, the primary chunk of your focus will be on Part 61 and Part 91. There are other pertinent parts, but these two contain the bulk of what you will need to know.

Instructors often sum up Part 61 is how to *get* your licenses, and Part 91 is how to *lose* them. While that is primarily true in a broad sense, you will learn there is more to it than that. To learn how to take charge of your training, I will focus now on Part 61.

Part 61 lists all the requirements you must meet and accomplish to take each check ride. The ACS provides a list of everything you need to *know* for each license, and Part 61 gives you a list of everything you need to *do* for eligibility to take each check ride.

Within Part 61, you will find subparts that pertain to each of the licenses you will be obtaining, starting with student pilot. Each subpart is broken into multiple sections.

For now, you will only care about the eligibility requirements, aeronautical knowledge, and aeronautical experience sections for each license.

Side note, instrument is not obvious to find in Part 61. A simple online search of "FAA regulation for instrument" can get you the correct regulation number you can then look up.

The eligibility requirement section is straightforward and lists prerequisites for each check ride, including but not limited to age restrictions, being proficient with the English language, and previous licenses you are required to have.

You can see that the eligibility requirements are extraneous to the realm of flying and knowledge required, which is why it is its own section. Nevertheless, you must meet these requirements, and those found in the aeronautical experience section, to be eligible to take the check ride they apply to.

The aeronautical knowledge section lists the topics you need to know before your instructor will sign you off to take your check ride. While these topics are mostly the same as those found in the ACS, the primary difference is that the items in the FARs are required for eligibility to take the check ride and the items listed in the ACS are what you will get tested on.

While these two lists are very similar, there are differences. I recommend you compare the FARs to the ACS to be thoroughly familiar with both.

The aeronautical experience section lists all the flight requirements you must complete before you are eligible to take the check ride. It will state how many cross-country flight hours you need, night hours, solo, etc.

Once you read through these sections for the license you are working on and combine them with the ACS, you will have a complete checklist of everything you need to know and do to be eligible for and pass your check ride. Now, it will be up to you to learn those things, accomplish the flying tasks, and be proficient in the flying maneuvers.

Think of the ACS and Part 61 as your course syllabus. If you ever feel like you do not know what you need to study or what you should be working on while flying, refer to the ACS's references page and Part 61 for a list of what you need to study and do. Study up on anything you do not know, accomplish all the flight requirements, and practice the flight maneuvers to the standards described in the ACS.

I cannot emphasize enough how important being familiar with the ACS and Part 61 is. They literally tell you everything you need to know and do.

Because you now know this, you should be taking the bull by the horns and telling yourself what you need to study and telling your instructor what tasks you need to accomplish and practice for each flight. Doing so will help you check off requirements quicker and maximize productivity with each flight hour, which saves you money.

You should never be in a position where you depend on your instructor to tell you what to study and what you will do during a flight. You already know your end goal is to get each license. So, if you use the ACS and Part 61 correctly, you will have the tools to come up with and know the exact path you need to take to reach that goal, know when you are ready to take the check ride, and can use your instructor as a facilitator to provide the tools you need to accomplish your goal.

It is now up to you to read through and use the ACS and Part 61 to develop your plan of action and inform your instructor of your plan and how they will help you execute it.

Stay focused on your goal, bare down, suck it up, stick with it, and accomplish your goal. The last and most important part is to enjoy the ride!

PART 61/141 CHECKLISTS

You are going to take the information you just learned to make some checklists that will organize all the requirements in a manner that will be beneficial to you throughout your training. I will creatively refer to them as the "Part 61/141 checklists."

The first step is reading through the aeronautical experience subpart of Part 61 that applies to private.

Next, create a checklist of all the flight requirements in a clear and distinguishable manner. However you go about it does not matter so long as you do it in a way that you have easy access to it and will see it often.

Include boxes you can check off next to each requirement. These boxes serve as a psychological boost of motivation each time you check one off and provide a visual for you to see your progress as it happens. Do not underestimate the positive reinforcement that checking off a to-do list can bring.

Then, do the same for instrument, commercial, CFI, CFII, and ATP. Yes, you are recreating the wheel in a sense, but it is going to be so much easier to refer to, you will be able to track your progress more efficiently, and you will receive a dopamine hit each time you check off a box giving you a nice boost of motivation.

If you are doing any courses under Part 141, obtain copies of the approved syllabi and create a checklist based on the syllabus for each course if the school does not already provide one.

If you have yet to decide if you will do Part 61 or Part 141, this is an excellent way to compare the two side by side to know which one has the least required flight and ground hours to know which will be cheaper.

Have each list side by side or in a manner that allows you to quickly compare each checklist without having to flip through pages of the FARs or changing screens. This way, you can see the requirements in a clear, concise, easy-to-read format that helps you differentiate the requirements for each license and provides a roadmap for your training.[1]

You will also notice there will be requirements that you can check off in a single flight and others that may take multiple flights, such as those for ATP, that you will have to work towards beyond your initial flight training.

Creating these checklists helps you to identify when, where, and how to implement two different strategies, both of which can help you save time and money.

The first strategy is recognizing when you can combine multiple flight categories into one flight to build up each category's overall total. Doing so will help you in the long run with working towards ATP.

The second strategy is finding requirements you can do in one flight that has the potential to fulfill checklist requirements simultaneously from other licenses you are not actively working on. These sound very similar, but I will break down the difference.

EFFICIENCY STRATEGY 1

To explain the first strategy of combining multiple flight categories, you first need to know what a flight category is.

Each flight you do has the potential for you to log 50+ pieces of information about that flight, or flight categories as I am calling them.

These flight categories can include the date of the flight, the location you took off from, the location you landed at, single-engine, multi-engine, airplane, rotorcraft, number of takeoffs and landings, night takeoffs and landings, day flight time, night flight time, cross-country, night cross-country, instruction received and so many more.

There are many ways to track these categories in the forms of physical logbooks and digital logbooks, each having their pros and cons.[2]

You will need a rudimentary understanding of cross-country, instrument, and night for some upcoming examples.

Cross-country is when you takeoff from one location and land at a different location. You may need a specified distance between the points depending on the situation and what you are working on.

Instrument is when you fly by referencing only your instruments inside the flight deck instead of relying on visual references outside. Instrument time can be actual or simulated.

Actual instrument is when you fly through clouds and cannot see outside the aircraft. Simulated instrument is when you can see outside the aircraft, but are using a view-limiting device, also known as a hood (usually in the form of blackout glasses) to prevent you from looking outside.

Night is exactly what it sounds like but has various definitions for when it begins and ends, based on what it is you are doing.

As you read through the regulations, you will learn that you are only required to log some flight categories, but not all. Nevertheless, the more flight categories you can track and log, the better. The more you have logged, the easier your life will be down the road as you apply to various jobs that want obscure flight categories such as night instrument. (While that example is a very obscure data point, I have had an employer ask for it).

By tracking multiple flight categories, you will have individual totals for each category that you can quickly reference. This way, you will not have to interpolate between or add and subtract multiple categories in an attempt to create a total for the category you are looking for, if that is even possible with what you have logged.

It is easier to log and track more categories starting with your very first flight than it is to go back later and try to add them in. By doing it this way, you will also avoid the possibility of falsifying documents with incorrect flight times, which can potentially get your licenses suspended or revoked. There is a slim chance of that happening, but it is possible.

You reap what you sow, and if you have not noticed yet, I am a big proponent of doing extra work on the front end, especially if it helps the back end exponentially more.

Now that you understand flight categories, I will return to the first strategy I mentioned and how to combine these categories per flight.

As you read through Part 61 and create your checklists, you will see requirements for x amount of cross-country time, x amount of night time, x amount of instrument time, and others for each license.

For example, as of writing this, ATP for airplanes requires you to have 500 hours of cross-country, 100 hours of night, 75 hours of instrument, and other requirements that are of no concern for this example. The minimum total flight time you would need to meet the above-listed requirements is 500 hours, not 675 hours (500 for cross-country, 100 night, and 75 instrument). This is because you can log multiple flight categories per flight. Here is an example.

If you were to do a single 3-hour flight that was cross-country, at night, while using a hood, you just accomplished 3 hours of cross-country, 3 hours of night, and 3 hours of instrument in one single flight.[3] However, you just flew 9 hours on paper even though you only flew for a total of 3 hours in the air.

In other words, you paid for 3 hours of flight time but knocked out 9 hours of flight time requirements by building up your cross-country, night, and instrument time towards ATP or any other license that needs x amount of each of those!

You can see how doing this is much more time and cost-efficient than if you did one 3-hour cross-country flight one day, the next evening did a second 3-hour night flight, and the following day did a third 3-hour flight under the hood. Going that route, you would pay for 9 hours of flight time over three different flights and take three days to accomplish the same thing you did in that one 3-hour flight! Pretty incredible, right?

Pro-tip, cross-country, night, and instrument are usually the most challenging flight categories for pilots to build time in when trying to meet ATP requirements. However, logistically, they are the easiest to combine and most often overlooked. If you start your training knowing this ahead of time and plan accordingly using the Part 61/141 checklists, you will be able to find all the times when you can combine as many flight categories into a single flight as possible.

While you are giddy to apply this strategy, you must know that you cannot do this for every flight. This especially rings true during private, where you will spend most of your time practicing various flight maneuvers for proficiency in the foundations of flying that you cannot do at night or under the hood for simulated instrument time.

The best time to combine multiple flight categories is during instrument training, specifically with night, cross-country, and simulated instrument.

Instrument will be the first and only license you can almost entirely accomplish at night. Additionally, aside from taxiing for takeoff and after landing, you can be under the hood for the entire duration of most flights. Therefore, you can easily combine night and simulated instrument time during almost every one of your flights while working on instrument. Then, depending on your situation, many of the flights can even be cross-country to get three for one!

But wait, there's more! (Thank you, Billy Maise). If combining night and simulated instrument flight categories per flight were not enough of a perk for you, you will also get the following benefits.

Flying at night helps build your proficiency with instrument flying as your outside visual references from peripheral vision decline at night, and you are more susceptible to experiencing actual spatial disorientation. Both add valuable, literal, life-saving experiences that will aid you in your flying career.

Look ahead and use the Part 61/141 checklists to use your flight time wisely and efficiently to take advantage of your instrument training to reap all the benefits you can.

EFFICIENCY STRATEGY 2

As you compare your Part 61/141 checklists side by side, you will notice times when requirements for one license are the same as another license, with the exception that one requires a further distance and/or duration.

Depending on the very specific circumstances involved, such as how the regulations are worded, the available legal interpretations put out by the FAA, and what your school allows, there *MAY* be the *POTENTIAL* to do a flight that accomplishes the longer duration and distance requirements and checks off the requirement for both flights. By doing this, you only pay for one flight but meet both requirements.

These scenarios are rare and require a thorough amount of research and a deep understanding of the regulations.

Due to the technicalities of everything involved and how the regulations and interpretations evolve, I will not provide any specific examples. I simply want to inform you of the potential for these scenarios and their ability to save you time and money. Your instructors should be able to provide more information on the matter.

Recap. Taking the time upfront to look ahead at the requirements for all the licenses, creating your Part 61/141 checklists, and applying these two strategies have the potential to save you the most time and money out of everything I teach you.

---

1. Be mindful that the requirements can change anytime, and your checklists can become outdated. The faster you get through each license, the slimmer the chance of that happening, but know it is possible.
2. Visit aviationlogbooks.com to purchase the most comprehensive physical pilot logbooks available!
3. Once you dig into the regulations, you will find you would not get 3.0 hours of simulated instrument time since there would be times during the flight when you cannot be under the hood. As such, it would be closer to 2.8 or 2.9 hours of simulated instrument time with this example, but the principle remains, and you get the idea.

17

THE BOOKS AND READING
LISTS

I am finally getting into the rest of the required books you will need to read throughout your training. I will start with some good news. They are all available for free from the FAA on faa.gov.

This is a good time to reiterate that the FAA came up with the rules you must play by to get all your licenses, and they will be testing you on the information they have published for free on their website. Faa.gov is also where to get the most up-to-date answers for you to study.

So again, you can either go straight to the source for everything you need with correct, complete, and current information you can easily reference later, or you can spend extra time and money reading third-party sourced information, your choice.

Most FAA books will have a reference number on the cover, such as FAA-X-XXXX-XX or AC XX-XX. This numbering system is the first giveaway that the FAA published the book.

You need to pay particularly close attention to the last two digits as they denote the version number of that book. How will you know if it is the current version or not? You guessed it, go to faa.gov and search the book.

In a moment, I will provide you with a list of the books you will need to read for each license, the corresponding reference number, and the most effective order for you to read them. As stated earlier, the lists I provide will NOT be a complete list of all referenced material you are required to know and be familiar with. My lists are the books that you should read first, as they will provide the bulk of the information you need to know. As such, these will be the books you will spend most of your time in and should prioritize.

Read through the books in the order listed unless specified otherwise. Start with the first, read it cover-to-cover, and then move on to the next. Reading in the order listed will help the topics build off each other more progressively than if you were to read them in a different order or bounce around from one book to the next.

You need to know the information in all the books, and the most efficient way to gain that knowledge is to read each book cover-to-cover in the order I am about to tell you.[1]

I recommend reading each book twice with at least a week to a month or so before reading the book a second time. Doing so will give you time to process and understand the information better. It will also allow you to get a few flights in that will further assist in understanding the information as you apply it while flying. However, do not hesitate to refer to the book whenever necessary.

You will be amazed at how much more you will get from each book the second time you read it. The more you read, talk about, and implement the things you are learning in practice, the more you will absorb, and the more everything will come together and make sense.

Now for the reading lists for each license that is current as of writing this.

PRIVATE

1. ACS - Private Pilot Airplane Airman Certification Standards: FAA-S-ACS-6B, **OR**
2. PTS - Private Pilot Practical Test Standards for Rotorcraft: FAA-S-8081-15A
3. Part 61/141 Checklists
4. POH/AFM
5. FAR/AIM
6. Pilot's Handbook of Aeronautical Knowledge (PHAK): FAA-H-8083-25B
7. Airplane Flying Handbook: FAA-H-8083-3C, **OR**
8. Helicopter Flying Handbook: FAA-H-8083-21B
9. Weight and Balance Handbook: FAA-H-8083-1B
10. Aviation Weather Handbook: FAA-H-8083-28
11. Remaining References

At this point, you know as much about the ACS as you can without reading it. With what you know, it should come as no surprise that the ACS will always be the first book you read for each license. Your goal with the ACS is familiarization, not memorization, so it should be a quick read.

Create your Part 61/141 checklists for each license through ATP using the FARs as discussed earlier. Do not worry about reading all the other regulations at this time. Hunker down and get the checklists created in one sitting. It should only take a couple of hours.

POH stands for Pilot Operating Handbook, and AFM stands for Approved Flight Manual. These are the equivalent of your car owner's manual. They apply to a specific make and model of aircraft and give you everything you need to know about the aircraft that separates it from other similar aircraft.

The easiest way to differentiate the two is that a POH is a type of AFM, and all aircraft are required to have an AFM. Because of the similarities, the two terms often get used interchangeably.

When you start flight training, you will get one or the other, depending on the aircraft you are flying. They both will have the same following chapter layout:

1. General Information
2. Limitations
3. Emergency Procedures
4. Normal Procedures
5. Performance Information
6. Weight and Balance
7. System Descriptions
8. Maintenance
9. Supplements

Read through the entire POH/AFM. There is a lot of detailed information that will help you get to know your aircraft. After you have read through it once, your next priority is to memorize all the emergency procedures and limitations. Flash cards will be your best friend here.

Focus on the emergency procedures first, then the limitations. If possible, try to have all the emergency procedures memorized before your first flight, but don't lose sleep over it if you come up short. You probably will not understand everything as you are initially memorizing them, but you will learn what each step references very quickly over the first few flights.

The sooner you memorize the emergency procedures, the better. Same with the limitations.

The emergency procedures will help keep you alive and the aircraft intact in the event of an emergency. The limitations will ensure the aircraft operates within normal parameters, which helps prevent emergencies. Both are good to know (massive under-exaggeration).

Here come the FARs again. Use the references page in the ACS to know which FAR parts you need to read through. It will give you the most comprehensive list of regulations you need to study. You can also use the suggested study list discussed earlier if you have access to it.

Remember, the suggested study list is a great place to start if you are overwhelmed by the number of regulations you need to study and want to break them down into more manageable bitesize chunks. However, the suggested study list does not have *all* the regulations you need to know.

The more familiar you are with the FARs and the more you have memorized, the better.

Have blank flashcards in hand as you read through new regulations for the first time. If you can easily remember the regulation and know where to find it by looking it up using the table of contents, don't worry about creating a flashcard. If the regulation is lengthy and has multiple rules, exceptions, limitations, or whatnot, make a flashcard for it right then and there. It will take longer to get through the regulations the first time around, but doing this will help you out more in the long run.

As you read, PAY ATTENTION TO EVERY WORD. The details matter. You need to know and understand each regulation, both the letter of the law and the spirit of the law.

You should approach your studying with the mentality that you will teach this one day. Because of this, even if a regulation does not apply specifically to you, read through it, understand it, know it exists, and know that you may need to refer to it again with your future students and potentially throughout your aviation career.

Pro-tip. As you read the regulations, occasionally stop to

look up the reg you just read using the table of contents. Think through how you would look it up had you just heard about it, had not read it before, and wanted to find it. Do this a handful of times to get used to looking up regs. It is another one of those small and simple things you can do right off the bat to help you build efficiency.

Due to the nature of the POH/AFM and the FAR/AIM and how much you need to memorize out of both, you will go back and forth to study them in short spurts throughout the whole time you work on each license. Thus, after you have read through the ACS and created your Part 61/141 checklists, you can study the POH/AFM and FAR/AIM in any order and at any time relative to the other books. Same with all the other licenses.

Any time you need a break from reading the other books, you should jump into the POH for the emergency procedures and limitations. Once you have those memorized, work on the FARs. These two will likely take longer to memorize than it will take to read through the other books, and as such, you need to be working on them throughout the same timespan you are reading the other books.

I recommend doing a chapter at a time when you begin reading through the POH/AFM and sticking with one part at a time while reading through the FAR/AIM. Going through and learning everything in clean chunks will help keep information more organized in your head and help ensure you do not skip over anything.

Read the Pilot's Handbook of Aeronautical Knowledge (FAA-H-8083-25B). Also known as the PHAK, this is the best introduction to everything you will need to know for private, commercial, and CFI.

It does a great job of providing an overview and relatively in-depth knowledge of almost all the major topics listed in the ACS. The PHAK covers information specific to both airplanes and rotorcraft. Yes, you should still read through the sections that discuss whichever aircraft you are not flying, as they will help later in training and with some of the knowledge tests.

The PHAK will probably take a couple of days to read through. It is a relatively easy read, but if you have never had any exposure to the information before, you may need to read things two or three times to get a better understanding of it, which adds time. If it takes you longer to get through this book, don't stress it.

Remember, all the information has to get into your head. If you are trying to get through it quicker than you can comprehend the information, you will not benefit from it, and it will slow you down. The lack of understanding will only exacerbate the confusion, which can cause frustration and despair. Take your time and understand what you read.

Up next is the Airplane Flying Handbook (FAA-H-8083-3C) or Helicopter Flying Handbook (formerly Rotorcraft Flying Handbook) (FAA-H-8083-21B), respective to whichever it is you are flying. There is no need to read both until you decide to add on the additional licenses to whichever you started with.

These books will provide more in-depth knowledge on the ins and outs of how the respective aircraft works mechanically and aerodynamically and other helpful topics. The subjects covered in these books will be more detailed than what is provided by the PHAK and will be a great addition to the PHAK.

Either of these books should take less time than it took for you to read the PHAK.

The Weight and Balance Handbook (FAA-H-8083-1B) is a relatively quick read and will teach you the principles of weight and balance and how to calculate both. The overall principles taught will carry over to every aircraft. However, do not be surprised when you find that your aircraft's weight and balance forms and charts look different than what you see in the book. The book teaches with a one-size-fits-all mentality, but in reality, every aircraft is unique.

Following the Weight and Balance Handbook is the Aviation Weather Handbook (FAA-H-8083-28). It will cover information such as aviation weather, thunderstorms, clear air turbulence avoidance, aviation weather services, pilot wind shear guidance, and hazardous mountain winds.

The Remaining References on my list include all the references listed in the ACS but not on my list. Use the references page found in the ACS to locate the additional remaining references. Look up each reference on faa.gov and read through them. For the most part, these references provide additional information to what you will have already read and are a great inclusion to your overall knowledge.

As a reminder, the DPE can use each reference listed in the ACS to come up with questions for the check ride, so do not skip over them.

To sum up, read through the ACS first, then create the Part 61/141 checklists, read the PHAK, Airplane/Helicopter Flying Handbook, Weight and Balance Handbook, Aviation Weather Handbook, and the additional remaining references. Start studying the POH/AFM and the FAR/AIM as soon as you finish the Part 61/141 checklists. Study them in chunks as you progress through the rest of the books.

When memorizing the emergency procedures, limitations, and FARs, the more repetitions you do, the better. The sooner you create flashcards for each, the easier it becomes to get those reps in, and the more prepared you will be for your check ride.

INSTRUMENT

1. ACS- Instrument Rating- Airplane Airman Certification Standards: FAA-S-ACS-8B, **OR**
2. PTS- Instrument Rating Practical Test Standards for Airplane, Helicopter, and Powered Lift: FAA-S-8081-4E
3. Part 61/141 Checklists
4. POH/AFM
5. FAR/AIM
6. Instrument Flying Handbook: FAA-H-8083-15B
7. Instrument Procedures Handbook: FAA-H-8083-16B
8. Remaining References

Start with the ACS cover-to-cover. Remember that this ACS is different than that used for private, so take a moment to ensure you are using the correct ACS by verifying the title and the license it applies to before you start reading through it.

Recall that the ACS is the new and improved PTS, and where both the ACS and the PTS for instrument include airplane in the title, you should default to the latest edition of standards available. As such, if you fly airplanes, you will use the ACS even though the PTS also says it includes airplanes.

You should already have your Part 61/141 checklists created, but this is a good time to review your checklist for accuracy and verify there were no updates in the regulations since you first made it.

You should be familiar with the POH/AFM now and how to study it unless you have changed the type of aircraft you train in. If you are using the same aircraft, read through the POH again to see if you can pick up something new you missed. If you are going to be flying in a different aircraft, go through the same process with the new POH/AFM that you did when you were working on private.

Use the references page in the ACS to know which FAR parts you need to read through. Again, the ACS will give you the most comprehensive list of FARs you need to study. You can also use the suggested study list discussed earlier if you have access to it.

Remember, the suggested study list is simply a great place to start if you are feeling a bit overwhelmed at the number of regulations you need to study and want to break them down into more manageable bitesize chunks. Nevertheless, the suggested study list does not necessarily have *all* the regs you need to know.

Just as you did with private, you can study the POH/AFM and FAR/AIM throughout the whole studying process after you have read through the ACS.

Read the Instrument Flying Handbook, followed by the Instrument Procedures Handbook. These two books work relatively the same as the PHAK and the Airplane/Helicopter Flying Handbooks in the sense that the Instrument Flying Handbook provides an excellent overview of what you will need to know for instrument, and the Instrument Procedures Handbook will go into greater detail and build off the Instrument Flying Handbook.

Once again, the reading list I provide excludes many references from the ACS reading list. The excluded references are grouped together on my list as "Remaining References."

Use the references page found in the ACS to locate the additional remaining references. Look up each one on faa.gov and read through them.

This time, many of the remaining references are duplicates from private, so most of it should be a review. Despite that, pay close attention as there are new references as well.

COMMERCIAL

1. ACS - Commercial Pilot Airplane Airman Certification Standards: FAA-S-ACS-7A, **OR**
2. PTS - Commercial Pilot Practical Test Standards for Rotorcraft: FAA-S-8081-16B
3. Part 61/141 Checklists
4. POH/AFM
5. FAR/AIM
6. Pilot's Handbook of Aeronautical Knowledge (PHAK): FAA-H-8083-25B
7. Airplane Flying Handbook: FAA-H-8083-3C, **OR**
8. Helicopter Flying Handbook: FAA-H-8083-21B
9. Weight and Balance Handbook: FAA-H-8083-1B
10. Aviation Weather Handbook: FAA-H-8083-28
11. Remaining References

In case you missed it, this is the same list I used for private, but now the Commercial ACS/PTS is included. This duplication is where you begin to see the concept of the two groups of licenses start to manifest.

Start with the ACS cover-to-cover, verify your Part 61/141 checklists are complete and current with any new regulation changes, and review and study the POH/AFM as necessary.

Refer to the ACS references page on what to study in the FAR/AIM. Part 119 is the additional topic you are required to learn for commercial that was not included in private. Part 119 is listed in the ACS but not the PTS, so ensure you include it in your studies.

You have already read the other books listed above. Nevertheless, read them again.

Having more experience now, you will get more out of each book this time than in previous times. Ensure you truly understand all the concepts. Any questions you have on topics should now be minor, and you should be able to explain the subjects without relying much on the book.

Once again, compare the reading list I provided to the ACS references page to identify and read through any remaining references not listed above.

If you have applied everything I have taught you up to this point, you should know the information at a CFI level. Don't panic if you are not quite there, though, as you still have time to get caught up. There is merely less time now between commercial and CFI than between private and CFI.

Pro-tip. To get CFI, you will need to create lesson plans that you will use to teach each topic covered in the private, commercial, and CFI ACSs. You will still need these lesson plans even if you can teach everything off the top of your head.

If you feel confident in yourself with your knowledge level and are further ahead than you need to be, this would be a great time to consider working on your lesson plans.

The lesson plans take an incredibly long time to create. Therefore, the sooner you start on them, the better, as long as you are not sacrificing your progress and preparation for the commercial check ride.

It is possible to buy premade lesson plans. While this saves a lot of time on the front end, I strongly advise against it because the creation process will be the best self-review you will get throughout flight training.

By creating your unique lesson plans, you will fill in any holes in your knowledge, know precisely what is in your lesson plans, and know all the information is correct.

If you go against my advice and buy lesson plans, ensure you review every piece of information to familiarize yourself with each lesson. Verify every single word and reference is current and correct, and practice teaching each lesson with the associated lesson plan to find any holes or missing information. Yes, this will be time-consuming, but it is what you need to do.

Not only is being able to teach everything vital because you are teaching things that will literally help keep people alive, but it will also be extremely obvious to the DPE if you are not familiar with your lesson plans when you go into your check ride. And because the DPE can ask you to teach any of the lessons, you need to know them all inside and out.

Remember that at this point in the training outline, you would be working on commercial. Because of this, you are not required to assemble your lesson plans yet.

Your primary goal and focus at this time should be passing the commercial check ride, and that is it. Only consider working on the lesson plans if you have accomplished everything else you need to for commercial and have extra time on your hands.

CFI

1. PTS- Flight Instructor Practical Test Standards for Airplane: FAA-S-8081-6D, **OR**
2. PTS- Flight Instructor Practical Test Standards for Rotorcraft: FAA-S-8081-7B
3. ACS - Commercial Pilot Airplane Airman Certification Standards: FAA-S-ACS-7A, **OR**
4. PTS - Commercial Pilot Practical Test Standards for Rotorcraft: FAA-S-8081-16B
5. ACS - Private Pilot Airplane Airman Certification Standards: FAA-S-ACS-6B, **OR**
6. PTS - Private Pilot Practical Test Standards for Rotorcraft: FAA-S-8081-15A
7. Part 61/141 Checklists

8. POH/AFM
9. FAR/AIM
10. Aviation Instructor's Handbook: FAA-H-8083-9B
11. Pilot's Handbook of Aeronautical Knowledge (PHAK): FAA-H-8083-25B
12. Airplane Flying Handbook: FAA-H-8083-3C, **OR**
13. Helicopter Flying Handbook: FAA-H-8083-21B
14. Weight and Balance Handbook: FAA-H-8083-1B
15. Aviation Weather Handbook: FAA-H-8083-28
16. Remaining References

This is the same list used for commercial and private with the addition of the Aviation Instructor's Handbook and the applicable PTS for CFI.

If you recall, there is an additional topic in CFI that was not included with private or commercial. That topic is FOI (fundamentals of instructing) and is found in the Aviation Instructor's Handbook.

FOI will take longer for you to learn than Part 119 did for commercial. Take your time with it and know it thoroughly, as the DPE will test you on it during the check ride.

As of writing this, the PTS is used for both airplane and rotorcraft CFI. Not the ACS. As a reminder, the FAA is phasing out the PTS, so by the time you read this, it may be the ACS for airplanes, rotorcraft, or both. There may also be a newer version of the ACS altogether.

At this point, you have figured out the process and know that the first thing you are going to do is read through the applicable CFI PTS cover-to-cover for the category of aircraft you fly.

Next, you will read through the ACS for both private and commercial for familiarization and as a review of what you need to know as you will teach both after obtaining CFI.

Review your Part 61/141 checklists for accuracy and

currency, study the POH/AFM as applicable, and study all the required FARs listed on the references page in each ACS/PTS for CFI, commercial, and private. They should all be mostly the same.

The new book you will be reading is the Aviation Instructor's Handbook. It provides an overview of what you need to know to obtain your CFI and teaches you all about the fundamentals of instruction.

From there, read through the other books listed above once more. It will be tempting not to, as you have already read them two or more times. However, you will find that you will still pick up new details each time you read through the books that you missed from prior times. This review will help you better know, understand, and teach each topic, making you more prepared for the CFI check ride.

You will want to be as on top of your game as possible for this check ride. CFI is typically the most failed check ride of them all. There is a myriad of reasons why people can fail a check ride, but the number one cause is a lack of preparation, necessary work, and studying required. There is no skirting by and "winging" this one. You will only pass this check ride if you put in the required work.

However, there is no need to stress or panic about it either. If you apply the principles I have taught in this book, do the necessary work, and thoroughly review each PTS/ACS as a final checklist to ensure you have not skipped over anything, you will be fine.

You will have already passed three other check rides, or possibly more for airplane pilots, so you will be familiar with the overall process and know what to expect. Like all the other check rides, the more prepared you are, the easier the check ride will be.

Once again, finish by comparing the reading list I

provided to the ACS' references page to identify and read through all the remaining references not listed above.

There is one more significant item you will need to complete before taking your CFI check ride, and that is compiling and assembling your lesson plans. The lesson plans are required and were discussed in the commercial reading list section if you need a review.

I recommend asking other instructors to see their lesson plans to get ideas on how to go about creating yours and how to organize them.

Including a table of contents that lists all the lessons logically with a page number will help significantly. You will not know which lesson(s) the DPE will have you teach. Therefore, you need to be capable of readily locating whatever lesson they choose. Not knowing which lesson they will choose again stresses the importance of creating your own lesson plans to know everything contained in them. Or, if you are going to buy them, you need to verify each piece of information is accurate, complete, and has the current and applicable references listed.

CFII

1. PTS- Flight Instructor Instrument Practical Test Standards for Airplane and Helicopter: FAA-S-8081-9D
2. ACS- Instrument Rating- Airplane Airman Certification Standards: FAA-S-ACS-8B, **OR**
3. PTS- Instrument Rating Practical Test Standards for Airplane, Helicopter, and Powered Lift: FAA-S-8081-4E
4. Part 61/141 Checklist
5. POH/AFM

6. FAR/AIM
7. Aviation Instructor's Handbook: FAA-H-8083-9B
8. Instrument Flying Handbook: FAA-H-8083-15B
9. Instrument Procedures Handbook: FAA-H-8083-16B
10. Remaining References

The above list is the same list I provided for instrument, with a couple of new additions.

You should definitely be familiar with the whole process by now, but I will run through it once more to hammer it in.

Just like CFI, as of writing this, both airplane and rotorcraft fall under the PTS for CFII. The PTS is being phased out, so by the time you read this, it may be the ACS for airplanes, rotorcraft, or both. There may also be a newer version of the ACS altogether.

Read through the applicable Flight Instructor Instrument PTS for the aircraft you fly. Since both airplane and rotorcraft are combined into this PTS, you only need to read the parts applicable to your aircraft category and then read through the applicable Instrument ACS/PTS as a review.

Review your Part 61/141 checklists for accuracy and currency, study the POH/AFM as applicable, and study all required FARs listed on the references page in the ACS/PTS for instrument and CFII. They should all be mostly the same.

Read through the Aviation Instructor's Handbook, Instrument Flying Handbook, and Instrument Procedures Handbook again. It will most likely have been a while since you last did this, as you were probably heavily focused on the first group of licenses while going through commercial and CFI.

Get spooled back up on everything. If you have taken my advice throughout this book and applied it to your training, your study habits will be solid, and you will know what to do.

Lastly, remember to check the ACS/PTS references page to read up on any remaining references not listed above.

This completes the reading lists for each of the basic licenses you will be acquiring through flight training. For those of you who will be flying airplanes and those of you who would like to add additional licenses to your repertoire, the same principles taught here will apply to any of the additional licenses you need or would like to acquire. Simply look up the applicable ACS/PTS, find the references page within to know what to read, look up the relevant section in the FARs for the flight requirements, and have at it.

Please note when obtaining add-on licenses, the hourly requirements are a little different. If you started with rotorcraft and are adding airplanes, you will have to do fewer flight hours in airplanes than you would if you had initially started in airplanes. This is because some of the time you have in rotorcraft will count towards the hourly requirements for airplanes, and vice versa. Read the regulations carefully to annotate these differences.

---

1. You can skip over some sections so long as they are obviously not applicable to the license you are working on. Specifically topics on multi-engine airplanes when you fly single-engine airplanes or rotorcraft. However, it is still a good idea to read everything as you never know when that information will come in handy or help supplement other topics.

18

KNOWLEDGE TESTS

For almost all your licenses, you will have to take a knowledge test. A knowledge test is a written, multiple-choice test taken at a designated testing facility and is commonly known as a written test. You must pass the knowledge test before being allowed to take the check ride.

Most knowledge tests require an endorsement from your instructor, and most instructors require you to show them multiple practice test scores with a minimum grade to sign you off. As long as you can obtain an endorsement if needed, you can take the knowledge test any time you would like.

Theoretically, you can take all the required knowledge tests for flight school before ever opening a book or taking your first flight. I recommend against this, but it is possible.

Once you take the knowledge test for a specific license, you will have 24 months to take the check ride for that same license. If the 24 months lapse before taking the check ride, you will need to retake the knowledge test and pay the fee again.

Because of that, most people will take each knowledge test

while working on the license it applies to, with an exception that I will discuss later.

Following that pattern, I highly suggest taking the knowledge test as soon as possible after starting each new license.

As of writing this, the knowledge tests are more of a nuisance than anything. There has been a rumor that the FAA is going to change the tests to make them more applicable and relative. However, for now, the best way to take and pass the knowledge test is by rote memorization. This means you need to memorize a large pool of questions and answers short-term, take the test, and then control-alt-delete the information from your memory.

The reason behind this is a good chunk of the questions in the pool that can be used on your test do not apply to the reality of flying. It sounds terrible, but that is just the way it is. For now.

The topics the questions are about are, for the most part, relevant topics that you do need to thoroughly know and understand. The issue is the way the questions are asked.

The way many of these questions are asked creates a scenario where you spend more time than you should trying to learn and understand the necessary topics from a quasi, bass-ackwards perspective. Whereas, if you were to simply rote memorize the pool of questions, take the test, and then move on, you could spend more time learning those same necessary topics, but from the reality and perspective you will use when flying.

Many of the test questions are poorly written at best. Others do not provide enough information to determine the correct answer, and some are flat-out wrong, where you must select an incorrect answer to the question asked to get it marked correctly on the test.

You can either let your pride get in the way and miss the question because you know what the correct answer is and select it, or you can accept reality and play the game by choosing the incorrect answer but getting it marked correct on the test.

There are many examples where the question will ask you something like, what is the VFR cloud clearance separation requirement at night in G airspace? Well, that depends. The answer is one thing for airplanes and another for rotorcraft, but the question does not tell you which it is asking about, and you will have both correct answers as options.

Yes, some knowledge tests will have questions about both airplanes and rotorcraft regardless of which aircraft you are flying, and you do need to know the correct answers to both, which is one more reason why rote memorizing the questions and answers for the knowledge test is more beneficial to the reality of flying.

Other questions approach the subject of the question so backward and illogical that it is practically impossible to understand what it is they are asking.

Then, there are the cross-country planning and weight and balance questions. You need to know how to complete these, and they are fantastic questions that truly test your knowledge. The problem is that they take up so much time to calculate that you generally do not have enough time to work through them and have enough remaining time to answer the rest of the questions.

There is another issue that arises from the good intent of studying, learning, and trying to make sense of these questions without the rote memorization part of it. That is, when you go in to take your test, the software system generates a test that pulls randomized questions from a large database, causing each test to be different. So, if you were to fail your first attempt and go back in a second time thinking you will now know the answers to the questions you missed, you will most likely have new questions to answer and run into the same style of terribly written questions that you did the first time.

Even if you knew everything there is to know about aviation, you would still miss multiple questions and could potentially fail because of it. How frustrating is that? Because of this, there are companies like Sheppard Air and ASA that provide test prep software for most of, if not all, the knowledge tests.[1]

For both companies, the test prep is simply a large pool of questions broken down into various organized topics that you go through and memorize before taking the test.[2]

Things change, so here is the same familiar disclaimer that the following information was current as of writing this.

Sheppard Air and ASA are the two primary providers of knowledge test prep software and provide the same overall service.

Sheppard Air provides a significantly smaller pool of questions to memorize and is updated more frequently. This means less time studying and more accurate questions. Sheppard Air will also give you a full refund if you have a surprise question on the test, which is a question that was not included in the test prep software. And depending on the test you are taking, they will offer a full refund if you get less than 90%. This refund is only available for one or two specific tests they provide test prep software for.

ASA provides a much larger pool of questions to memorize, as many as 400-500 more questions than Sheppard Air, but they do NOT offer refunds for surprise questions or guaranteed scores. However, they are considerably cheaper.

Both are effective and accomplish the same task. The big difference is, when taking your test, would you rather take longer, put in more work, and save money, or would you rather pay more, save time, and have a better guarantee?

You may also opt to use a different company or no study

prep at all. It is entirely up to you. However, while instructing full-time, I would only sign off my students to take a written test if they used a test prep program and showed me at least three practice tests with scores over 90%. I know that most other instructors are the same way.

Sheppard Air and ASA are set up similarly and can do practice tests in different formats with different options. While ASA and Sheppard Air might not have all the following testing formats and options, these are the general setup choices while working on your practice tests.

The first format will generate a test that shows the questions in a set order and shows only the correct answer. The second format will create a test that shows the questions in a set order and displays all the multiple-choice answers you can choose from in a specified order. The third format will generate a test with the questions in mixed order, but the answers are in the same set order as before for each question. The fourth format will populate a test with both the questions and the answers in a mixed order.

There are two options you can choose regarding how many questions are generated on the practice tests. The first is to create a test with the same number of questions relative to the specific knowledge test you are studying for, and the second option is to show the entire pool of questions in the database for the test prep software. You can choose either option when studying for one specific topic or a comprehensive test including all the topics.

For example, if you are studying aerodynamics, and the knowledge test you are preparing for asks only 15 aerodynamic questions, your practice test will only generate 15 questions on aerodynamics. Or, you can choose the entire database of aerodynamic questions from the test prep software, which could be 50 or more questions.

The same principle applies when practicing a comprehensive test. Suppose the knowledge test you are preparing for has 75 total questions. In that case, you can use the test prep software to generate a 75-question test with mixed topics, or you can have the software create a test that includes the entire pool of questions for all topics, which can easily be 600 questions or more.

As confusing as this might sound, once you can play around with the test prep software of your choice, you will be able to figure it out quickly.

Take two to three days and dedicate them to studying only the test prep software and nothing else related to aviation. Because of how you study for the knowledge test compared to flying, you will want to keep these two types of studying separate and keep your preparation for the knowledge test as condensed as possible.

The following is the most beneficial way I have found to go about studying for the knowledge tests and very closely matches the steps that Sheppard Air will tell you to do as well.

Start with an individual topic. The first time you run through the questions for that topic, select the option to see the question and the correct answer only. This is where the law of primacy (what you learn, see, or hear first sticks best) will become your best friend. Read the question thoroughly and then read the answer thoroughly. Read the question and answer twice, and ignore the letter the answer corresponds to (a, b, or c) as they will change on the actual test.

If you understand the question and the answer makes sense, great. The question will be that much easier to remember. If not, don't stress it, don't think about it too hard, just read the question and answer, and then move on to the next question.

Once you have gone through all the questions on that topic, do the same topic again, but this time, select the option to see the questions and all the answers. The questions will appear in the same sequence, and the correct answers may appear as the same selection (a, b, or c) as before, but again, ignore the letter as it may be different on the actual test!

When you run through the topic this time, you will be surprised at how well your brain helps you pick out the correct answer due to the law of primacy. Even with the questions you are unsure of.

Go with your initial gut instinct, as it is usually right. You will likely still miss a few, but you will get the majority correct. If you get less than 70% on this run-through, repeat the same topic with the same settings. Otherwise, move on to the next step.

Now, with the same topic as before, select the option to see both the questions and answers in random order. This time, all the questions will be in random order, and the answers will be in a different order as well. If you get above 85%, I recommend moving on to the next topic, but if you want to run through the same topic again, go for it. More reps will not hurt. It will just take more time.

Repeat the same process with each topic. Once complete, set up a practice test that has every question from every topic in random order using the entire pool of questions.

At this point, you will have already seen each question three times minimum, so it should be relatively easy. If you do well on the test with every question in the pool, then you should be good to go for the knowledge test.

For me, if I did well on the first run-through with all the questions in the database, I would do a second run-through of all the questions and then take the test if the testing center was still open. If the testing center was already closed, I would hold off on the second run-through until first thing in the morning and then immediately take the test.

Once the test is complete, put the pool of questions behind you. There is no reason to look at them anymore. Yes, private, commercial, and CFI cover most of the same material you need to know to pass the check ride, but the pools of questions for the knowledge tests are entirely different.

So once again, after you have completed your knowledge test, put it behind you and get back to reality with the rest of your studying.

The exception to this is for instrument, CFII, and IGI (instrument ground instructor). These three tests use the same pool of test questions and can all be knocked out one after the other on the same day.

Remember, things can change, so first verify that they all still use the same pool of questions before you try to take them all at once. Also, remember that you will have 24 months to complete the instrument and CFII check rides before you will have to retake the knowledge test. Therefore, do not plan on taking the CFII knowledge test at the same time as the instrument knowledge test unless you are sure you can get both check rides done within 24 months.

IGI does not require a check ride, so once the knowledge test is complete, there are no timelines to worry about. You will simply need to schedule an appointment with the FAA to show them that you completed the test, and they will issue your license.

Approaching your knowledge tests in this manner is by far the quickest and easiest way to prepare for and know that you will pass each test.

Again, take two to three full days to complete this process with each knowledge test. If you work a full-time job or family life dictates it will take more than two to three days, no worries. The main idea here is to study nothing but the test prep software for the duration you are working on it and complete it in the shortest time possible.

The less time it takes to run through this whole process, the easier it will be to memorize the answers via the law of primacy, the better you will do on your test, and the sooner you can put it behind you. It will take much longer and be so much more challenging to prepare for and pass the knowledge tests if you chop up the studying over an extended period and study other material between.

You may think you can run through the questions once or twice and still pass, and you probably wouldn't be wrong. I have known many individuals who did something similar. Some did quite well, and others were completely content passing with a minimum score. After all, passing is passing.

It is possible to successfully graduate from flight school with all your licenses in hand with that mentality, but that is short-term over long-term thinking and goes against the principles I have been teaching you. It gets you through the first gate but does not grease the skids for down the road.

I have had multiple employers ask about knowledge test scores along with stage checks and check ride failures. I am sure you will as well. While it is common for most pilots to have a failure or two and a lower-than-desired test score, would you rather report in an interview that your average test score was just above or well above passing?

How fun do you think it would be to say you failed a knowledge test or a check ride? What about having to explain in an interview that the reason you failed was you did not put in the necessary work or study as well as you should have to pass the first time? Or how would you feel about lying and saying you failed because of something else? How do you think that makes you look to the employer?

Chances are getting a job will not come down to your test scores alone. Nevertheless, your whole mentality towards aviation and life should always be to put your best foot forward and strive for the highest level of success in all you do.

Remember that every time you apply for a job, you are

selling yourself. So why sell yourself short by accepting the minimum?

---

1. I am not getting paid by either ASA or Sheppard Air.
2. This solves the problem of terribly written questions and helps you jump through the hoop to check the box. But all it is doing is testing your ability to memorize aviation-related information that is not all practical or useable in the real world.

✤ 19 ✤
THE DPE

Designated pilot examiners will conduct your check ride on behalf of the FAA. Each check ride has a cash fee the DPE charges for their time and services. The rate varies based on the license you are working on and is set by each DPE.

As you can imagine, there can be a wide array of emotions if a failure occurs during a check ride, and in the past, people have skipped out on paying the DPE. Because of this, it is customary to pay the DPE as soon as you sit down with them to begin the check ride.

Unbeknownst to most new pilots, you do not have to use any specific DPE. Many flight schools will have one or more preferred DPEs they use. This can be due to the DPE's rate, previous good experiences, personal relationships, etc. These DPEs maintain an unwritten status with the flight schools based on previous experiences and pass rates.

The flight schools want you to pass your check ride to help advertise high success rates. If a DPE is known to fail numerous students over petty things or overcharges, their relationship with the school may waiver. Because of this, more often than not, the DPE recommended by the school is a good choice.

If, for whatever reason, you prefer not to use the suggested DPE, you are free to use whichever DPE you like. I recommend speaking with your instructor and other students to get an idea of which DPE you want to use. Beyond that, you can find a list of all the DPEs on faa.gov and call each to find out their price, availability, and whether you need to go to them or if they will be willing to come to you.

Pro-tip. Use whichever DPE is known for being the easiest. Failing will bruise your ego and cost you more money. Additionally, many companies require you to list your failures on applications, which further bruises the ego. This is the one time I will advise you to take the easiest path possible by finding the DPE you have the best chance of passing with.

The biggest piece of advice I can give you for the oral evaluation of the check ride is to answer the DPE's questions to the extent they ask it. This means that if you can answer the question with a simple yes or no, answer with ONLY yes or no.

At this point in your training, you will have learned a lot and may have a strong desire to demonstrate your knowledge on the subject asked about. Set your pride aside and refrain from doing this.

If you start offering additional information beyond what the DPE asks, you may end up volunteering incorrect information beyond the answer they were looking for. This exposes chinks in your armor (weakness in your knowledge), and for safety reasons, depending on how incorrect the information you provided was, the DPE will then use that volunteered information to generate follow on questions.

Similar to cutting out the rotten part of an apple, the DPE uses this to find out just how much you do not know about a specific topic. As you can see, this is a rabbit hole you do not want to go down voluntarily.

Help yourself by sticking to the minimum necessary information that fully answers the question asked. Nothing more, nothing less.

Know this. The DPE wants you to pass. They are not a bad person there to destroy your hopes and dreams and feed off your tears of failure. Do not overthink it.

Stay relaxed in the check ride. Approach it with the mentality that you are conversing with a fellow aviation enthusiast because, ultimately, that is what you are doing.

Exceed the standard throughout your training so that meeting the standard on check ride day is easy. There is no reason to stress about the check ride because stress comes from a lack of preparation, and if you have applied what you have learned in this book, you will be well prepared to exceed the expected standards.

20

WHERE TO SPECIFICALLY
SAVE TIME AND MONEY

SAVE TIME

1. Attend a flight school in a geographical location that has sunny days the majority of the year - The tradeoff is less real-world experience in looking up various weather products and making the critical go/no-go decision with actual weather
2. Use the Part 61/141 checklists you create to come up with a plan and the order in which you want to complete each task, track your progress, and reduce redundancy - Fewer flights equal less time (and money) to complete your training
3. Focus on completing the requirements first, refine proficiency second - This ensures requirements are met by the time you feel ready for the check ride and minimizes any delays
4. Only read and study the books and references listed in the ACS/PTS - Every additional resource you read adds more time

5. Take the knowledge test for the license you are working on sooner rather than later - This prevents delaying taking the check ride if you have already met all the other requirements

6. Reduce distractions when reading and studying - Turn off your phone or put it in another room, find a quiet place to study with minimum movement in your peripheral vision, and read and study as often as possible

7. Fly frequently to gain proficiency faster - It takes less flight time (and total time) to be ready for a check ride

8. Chair fly - Sit in a chair, close your eyes, and go through all the motions of moving the controls and switches while imagining what the aircraft should be doing in response to your inputs

SAVE MONEY

1. Use the Part 61/141 checklists you create to come up with a plan and the order in which you want to complete each task, track your progress, and reduce redundancy - Fewer flights equal less money (and time) to complete your training

2. Focus on completing the requirements first, refine proficiency second - This ensures requirements are met by the time you feel ready for the check ride and minimizes any delays

3. Chair fly often - Especially when learning new maneuvers or when you need extra practice with tasks or a better understanding of everything that is happening with whatever it is you are working on

4. Set up a camera inside the aircraft and record your flights so that you can review what was said and what happened - Ensure you only use the camera as a training tool while in flight training, not for social media

5. Utilize your flight time as efficiently as possible - Plan the details of each flight before you takeoff

6. Know precisely what you are going to do on each flight and in what order

7. Have more planned than you can accomplish in a single flight to avoid wasting time in the aircraft while trying to decide what else you would like to work on

8. Communicate your plan to your instructor BEFORE getting to the aircraft so they know your intentions and can help facilitate the plan

9. Know exactly where you are going to go and reduce commute time to other airports or designated practice areas by choosing the closest location(s) possible

10. Make good use of the commute time by going over questions or having your instructor test you on ground knowledge, such as quizzing emergency procedures, limitations, and regulations

11. If taking off at a place known for heavy air traffic, schedule your flights during the times with the least amount of air traffic to avoid the "rush hour" equivalent at an airport - This prevents paying for time sitting on the taxiway waiting to takeoff and/or flying in a holding pattern while waiting to get back into the airport

12. Combine flight categories and flight requirements into each flight whenever possible

13. Read with the intent to teach and vocalize everything - This helps you learn how to teach for when you become an instructor, better understand the information if you do not become an instructor, may help answer some of your questions as you talk through it, and you may come up with further questions that will help you understand the topic even more once you find the answers

14. Read, discuss, and implement what you read and learn - If you are still uncertain about the topics you are learning and cannot get a free answer, then pay for ground instruction, but only when you actually need it

15. Take charge of your training by telling your instructor when you need ground, not them telling you - The caveat is if your course is Part 141 as ground instruction is required

16. If your instructor suggests ground, but you are progressing as you should and feel that you are on course to succeed, do not be afraid to say so and have a discussion on it - Articulate where you stand with measurable information, such as what books you have and have not read to show that you are progressing at an appropriate pace on your own

17. Remind your instructor that you are the one paying for your training and are trying to save as much money as possible

21

STEPS TO ACQUIRE EACH LICENSE

CONDENSED ORDER OF EVENTS

READ THE ACS/PTS

- Lists everything you need to know for the check ride
- States the standards for each maneuver
- Lists all the references you need to know, read, and be familiar with, including the FAR/AIM references you need to study

CREATE THE PART 61/141 CHECKLISTS FOR EACH LICENSE

- Used to track your progress and reduce potential redundancy in training, which saves you money
- Part 61 checklists will come from the FARs
- Part 141 checklists will come from the approved syllabi

ACTUALLY READ THE BOOKS AND REFERENCES LISTED IN THE ACS/PTS

- Read with the intent to teach, not just understand

READ THROUGH AND MEMORIZE THE POH/AFM

- Can be studied anytime throughout the process
- Memorize the emergency procedures first, then the limitations

STUDY THE FAR/AIM REFERENCES FROM THE ACS/PTS AND MEMORIZE THE REGS

- Can be studied anytime throughout the process
- Study one part at a time to avoid skipping regulations

TAKE THE KNOWLEDGE TEST

- Can be studied and taken anytime throughout the process
- Take 2-3 days to study nothing but the test prep software
- Do one topic at a time with only the right answers first, then mixed answers, then mixed questions and mixed answers, then a test with the entire pool of questions with mixed questions and mixed answers
- Immediately go take the test
- Control + alt + delete the information

USE YOUR CHECKLISTS

- Complete all required tasks on your Part 61/141 checklist
- Use the ACS/PTS as a final checklist to verify you know all the information about each item listed

TAKE THE CHECK RIDE

- Answer only what the DPE asks - no more, no less
- Pass the check ride
- Rinse and repeat

CONCLUSION

YOU ARE IN CHARGE OF YOUR TRAINING AND FUTURE

"All good thoughts and ideas mean nothing without action."

— MAHATMA GANDHI

You now know what you do not know, and it is up to you to learn it. You are paying for your training. Get what you need from it. Learn what the requirements and standards are and use that knowledge to know what you still need to accomplish and what you need to work on.

Show up to each ground and flight lesson prepared, knowing exactly what you want to work on and accomplish. Brief your instructor on the plan of action for the day. Focus on knocking out the requirements first and finessing proficiency second. Use your flight time wisely and efficiently to maximize productivity, which will decrease you expenses. Only pay for ground when you need it.

Consider each license you obtain a license to learn. Just

because you get the license does not mean you know everything about it. Be patient, be humble, and always strive to learn as much as possible.

You got into aviation for a reason, remember why. If you are getting overwhelmed in training, do not be afraid to ask for a fun flight from time to time to remove the stress of learning, enjoy the scenery, and just fly.

The ball is in your court, and I have taught you how to maximize efficiency. You now have the knowledge and ability to navigate and take charge of your training. You know how, when, and where to save the most time and money, allowing you to be as efficient with your training as possible. How closely you follow this path is entirely up to you.

It is up to you to put in the required work. You will get what you put into it. The quality of the pilot you become will largely depend on the quality of the student you are. The path may not be easy, but it will be worth it.

Congratulations again on taking the first steps to becoming a pilot!

Thank you for taking the time to read Becoming A Pilot! For updates on upcoming books and the opportunity to interact with other pilots in training, please join our Facebook group, Becoming A Pilot.

If you enjoyed this book or found it helpful, please take a moment to leave a favorable review and be sure to tell other new pilots how they too can benefit from the contents as they accomplish their dreams of:

BECOMING A PILOT

OTHER GREAT PRODUCTS FROM
JAMES D KOFFORD

Visit aviationlogbooks.com to purchase the most comprehensive physical pilot logbooks available.

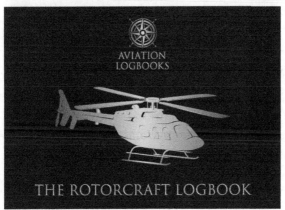

❧ 23 ❧

BECOMING A PILOT
ABBREVIATED

BEFORE YOU START TRAINING

- Obtain a first-class medical

FLIGHT SCHOOLS

- Do your due diligence and research
- What is the cost?
- What is the weather like year round?
- Will you be able to fly and receive ground instruction at the pace and frequency you are hoping for?
- Part 61 or Part 141?
- What is the networking potential?
- Be comfortable with the cost
- Make a decision and get started

YOUR INTERVIEW ALREADY STARTED

- You are subconsciously being watched and evaluated by those you interact with
- Be aware of yourself, your actions, and your surroundings
- Be the person you would want to hire
- You are guilty by association because perception is reality, and first impressions last the longest

INSTRUCTORS

- Instructors are not equal
- Interview instructors to fill the teacher role you are hiring for
- You might not choose your instructor, but you can choose what you do about them

MORE THAN JUST FLYING

- Read from the source for complete, accurate information
- Study, memorize, teach, repeat

OVERVIEW OF LICENSES

- Private
- Commercial
- Instrument
- CFI
- CFII

TESTING COMPONENTS OF A LICENSE

- Prerequisites
- Knowledge requirements
- Flight experience requirements and skills
- Stage checks, if applicable
- Written test
- Check ride

PROGRESSING THROUGH TRAINING EFFICIENTLY

- Have the entire flight planned out before getting into the aircraft
- Fly frequently
- Keep your knowledge progressing equal to or faster than your flying, read all the required material, study often
- For every hour of flight, spend at least two hours studying
- Look ahead at the requirements for all the licenses, not just the license you are working on

STAYING FOCUSED ON THE GOAL

- Prioritize what you study
- Study only what you need to
- Read the other resources after you have your licenses

THE RIGHT MENTALITY AND LEARNING TO TEACH

- Study with the mentality you are going to become an instructor
- Learn with the intent to teach what you read, not just understand
- Paint the picture as you teach
- Vocalize everything in and out of the aircraft

HOW TO APPROACH STUDYING

- Use the ACS and FAR Part 61 or the approved Part 141 syllabus to find what you need to know and do
- Actually read each book from the source (FAA) to get complete, accurate information and know where to reference it
- Read, discuss, and implement each topic
- Avoid study groups unless you have already read and have a basic understanding of the information you will be discussing

FAA.GOV

- Use this to find everything you need
- Contains the most current version of each publication
- Everything is free

THE ACS

- Contains a list of everything you need to know and be able to expound upon
- Contains the standards you must fly your maneuvers to
- Contains a references page with everything you need to read and be familiar with

THE FAR/AIM

- FARs are made up of many parts, subparts, sections, and subsections
- AIM is made up of chapters that elaborate on the FARs and how to operate in the National Airspace System
- Part 61 lists all the requirements you must meet to be eligible for each check ride
- Use the ACS references page to know which regulations and AIM chapters to study

THE BOOKS AND READING LISTS

- The lists contained herein provide the books you should prioritize and read first
- Ensure you read and are familiar with the remaining references listed on the ACS references page
- All references listed in the ACS are fair game for the DPEs to draw questions from

KNOWLEDGE TESTS

- Most require an endorsement
- Can be taken at any time
- Have a fee associated with them
- Use test prep software to study
- Take 2-3 days to study nothing but the test prep software, take the test, and move on

THE DPE

- Representative of the FAA
- Pay upfront each time you start a check ride or retest
- Can choose whichever DPE you would like to use
- Find the easiest DPE you can
- Answer only what they ask, nothing more, nothing less

SOURCES

- *Aviation Logbooks*. (n.d.). https://aviationlogbooks.com
- *Private Pilot's License – Zone Aviation*. (n.d.). http://www.zoneaviation.com/learn-to-fly/private-pilots-license/
- *Lee Atwater Quotes*. (n.d.). BrainyQuote. https://www.brainyquote.com/quotes/lee_atwater_409179
- Federal Aviation Administration. (n.d.). *Federal Aviation Administration*. Retrieved November 9, 2022, from https://www.faa.gov
- Federal Aviation Administration. (2016, August 24). *Pilot's Handbook of Aeronautical Knowledge, FAA-H-8083-25B*. https://www.faa.gov/aviation/phak/pilots-handbook-aeronautical-knowledge-faa-h-8083-25b
- Federal Aviation Administration. (2022, November 8). *Airman Certification Standards*. https://www.faa.gov/training_testing/testing/acs
- Federal Aviation Administration. (2022, November 8). *Practical Test Standards (PTS)*. https://www.faa.gov/training_testing/testing/test_standards
- Emmerich, R. (Director). (2000, June 27). *The Patriot*.
- Hope, M. (2022, July 12). *"Chance Favors the Prepared Mind" - Conquer Destiny*.

Asymmetric. https://asymmetric.pro/chance-favors-the-prepared-mind/

- *Sheppard Air Flight Test 5.0 Prep Software ATP, Flight Engineer, Mil Comp - FAA Airline Transport Pilot.* (n.d.). https://www.sheppardair.com
- Wachowski, L., & Wachowski, L. (Directors). (1999). *The Matrix.* Warner Bros., Village Roadshow Pictures, Groucho Film Partnership, Silver Pictures, 3 Arts Entertainment.
- Repository, S. W. C. (2010, September 12). Reference to 'teaching a man to fish' isn't from Bible. *The Repository.* https://www.cantonrep.com/story/opinion/letters/2010/09/12/reference-to-teaching-man-to/986125007/

Made in the USA
Las Vegas, NV
29 November 2024

12871657R00095